The Chronicles

of

Connie

by

Constance Cooper

The Chronicles of Connie

Copyright: Constance Cooper
March 20, 2011

ISBN 13: 978-1461077626
ISBN 10: 1461077621

For information or to contact the author:
CONSTANCE COOPER
connieantioch@yahoo.com
www.TheChroniclesOfConnie.weebly.com

Unless otherwise noted, all scripture references are from the New International Version (NIV) of the Bible.

Printed in the USA
Published by: Tranzform-N-U Publications
Cover design: Areli MediaWorks
Cover photographs by: Curtis Jermany, GZphotoZ.com

~ *Table of Contents* ~

When I came to you, brothers, I did not come with eloquence or superior wisdom as I proclaimed to you the testimony about God. For I resolved to know nothing while I was with you except Jesus Christ and him crucified. I came to you in weakness and fear, and with much trembling. My message and my preaching were not with wise and persuasive words, but with a demonstration of the Spirit's power, so that your faith might not rest on men's wisdom, but on God's power. We do, however, speak a message of wisdom among the mature, but not the wisdom of this age or of the rulers of this age, who are coming to nothing. No, we speak of God's secret wisdom, a wisdom that has been hidden and that God destined for our glory before time began. None of the rulers of this age understood it, for if they had, they would not have crucified the Lord of glory. However, as it is written: "No eye has seen, no ear has heard, no mind has conceived what God has prepared for those who love him" — but God has revealed it to us by his Spirit. The Spirit searches all things, even the deep things of God. For who among men knows the thoughts of a man except the man's spirit within him? In the same way no one knows the thoughts of God except the Spirit of God. We have not received the spirit of the world but the Spirit who is from God, that we may understand what God has freely given us. This is what we speak, not in words taught us by human wisdom but in words taught by the Spirit, expressing spiritual truths in spiritual words. The man without the Spirit does not accept the things that come from the Spirit of God, for they are foolishness to him, and he cannot understand them, because they are spiritually discerned. The spiritual man makes judgments about all things, but he himself is not subject to any man's judgment: "For who has known the mind of the Lord that he may instruct him?" But we have the mind of Christ. --1Corinthians 2:1-16

~ *Dedications* ~

This book is dedicated to my late father Tom Cooper. I miss you and love you dad.

I would also like to dedicate this book to my beautiful mother, Shirley Carson, I love you. You shaped me into the woman I am today. You are truly a queen. You worked hard to make sure my sisters and I had the best of everything. We lacked no good thing coming up. My children: Eric, Najee, Alex, and Raven. All of you have loved mommy at every level of life we were on. There are no words for the joy all of you bring to my life everyday. I love you all so much.

~ *Acknowledgements* ~

First and always I thank my Lord and Savior, Jesus Christ. I love The Holy Trinity, They have always had my back. Without Them I would have never finished this assignment. Yes, in life you will always have assignments. That's our Father and He never changes but this world does. We are supposed to be forever learning and growing. The Word of God reads, "My people perish for lack of knowledge." To me that means we will never stop learning or growing until we see Him face to face.

Of course I give a special thank you to my pastor and spiritual father, Pastor Kirkland A. Smith and First Lady Quivander Smith. They are two of the most phenomenal people I have ever met and they have a powerful ministry that loves, encourages, nourishes, and nurtures. It teaches and inspires you to want to know more about this true love with Jesus. Pastor Smith, each time you allowed the Lord to use you, it pushed me to want to discover everything that God planned for my life. Every bible study got me over the hump, helped me cross those crossroads when you don't know what or which way to go. The very words that God gave you catapulted me to the next level of where God wanted me. I was broken a few times during this project and my life's journey. Thank you, thank you, thank you.

The next person I'm about to mention, who I call my spiritual mother, is Pastor Phyllis Scott. What can I say about her but thank you and I love you. She always told me from the beginning that I was a minister. She has encouraged me and said, once God has called, it doesn't matter what man says. She helped me understand that "the harvest was ripe but the laborers are few," and there was a special flock that I was especially designed for. Thank you Pastor Scott and The Tree Of Life Empowerment Ministry family.

To Reverend Joan Wright Richardson, whom I have had the pleasure to know and love for the past 6 years, this is my sister in Christ. She knows the lonely dark places I had been in. She knew when I fell, when I was up, when I was happy and when I was sad. I love Joan. She was my first accountability partner and she told me how to confess my sins so the enemy wouldn't get any more footholds in my life. I do have a few words for you sister girl... you are a breath of fresh air to the Kingdom. I can't wait to see and hear your gifts to this world. Let's make Daddy proud Sis.

To my spiritual grandfather, Pastor Harold R. Mayberry—this man took me in and showed me the love of

Christ. He helped me to understand the word and how to study. He told me that Jesus loved me the way I was, and that He would make me whole.

There are others to thank, but as the Word of God reads: now the first shall be last and last shall be first. Pastor Mayberry, you always told me that God would use me if I just kept pushing and never give up. Well you were right because here is the baby I was in labor with for the past five years. I love you and the entire First A.M.E. family.

Thank you to my enemies because without the haters I wouldn't have kept calling on that name Jesus. You too are loved by God, for we are all His children.

~ Foreword ~

And they overcame him by the blood of the Lamb, and by the word of their testimony; and they loved not their lives unto the death. --Revelations 12:11

In the early fall of 2010, I received a request from one of the commentary writers of the weekly news publication I work for. He knew a young lady by the name of Constance Cooper who was interested in publishing a book. Since I was a new author, he wondered if I wouldn't mind sharing how to self publish or at least forward Ms. Cooper to the resources that would help her achieve her goal. So I sent an email to her outlining in detail the steps I took to finish my book and I thought that would be the end of it. But after a few back and forth contacts via email, she and I eventually conversed with one another by telephone. It turned out to be the most enlivening conversation that ended in both of us praying for one another.

Through subsequent conversations with Constance, I came to know that my first impression of her humility and sincerity was truly genuine. I agreed to at least copyedit her manuscript before forwarding her on to other resources for the publishing process.

I received her manuscript a few days later and decided to look at it the next day when I had free time. Despite being tired from a long day at work, curiosity got the best of me. So around 2:00 a.m., I decided to read just the introduction. I could not put it down! The anointing flew off the pages. As I read the manuscript I could feel that God had His mighty hand on Constance's hand as she typed her testimony. I know that God has people in hidden places, who have been tried, broken, mended, restored to ultimately be revealed to the Body of Christ. These men and women who have submitted their lives to the processing of the Holy Spirit will be those that He uses to enlarge His Kingdom.

Ms. Constance Cooper is such a one who God is going to use to instill hope in a generation of people who thought themselves hopeless. This book "The Chronicles of Connie" is a vehicle from the vessel that will by the enabling power of the Holy Spirit, break yokes and set the captive free. Matthew 10:8 says that our reasonable service as the believer is to... *Heal the sick, cleanse the lepers, raise the dead, cast out devils: freely ye have received, freely give* (KJV). We all as believers have been given the ministry of reconciliation...*And all things are of God, who hath reconciled us to himself by Jesus Christ, and hath given to us the ministry of reconciliation.* –2 Corinthians 5:18 KJV.

Constance has revealed her diligence in evangelistically serving the Lord through her obedience in writing this book. She fearlessly tells the story of her life with a transparency about the struggles and the victories that is truly captivating. Throughout the pages, she gives all glory to the Lord God for all things, even for what is to come. For she knows and acknowledges that her times and seasons are in the hands of the Lord and He is yet making her to become what He has planned, purposed and destined for her life. To my spiritual daughter Constance: This is true humility, and if retained, it will take you to places, realms and dimensions that you have yet to fathom. *Being confident of this very thing, that he which hath begun a good work in you will perform it until the day of Jesus Christ.* --Philippians 1:6 KJV

And finally, to every reader of "The Chronicles of Connie," expect your miracle, healing and deliverance and your expectation shall not be cut off. *For surely there is an end; and thine expectation shall not be cut off.* --Proverbs 23:18 KJV.

Christine Brooks Martin

Author of "Pray What God Says"

Production Manager, Los Angeles Sentinel Newspaper

~ *Foreword* ~

Romans 8:1-3

Therefore, there is now no condemnation for those who are in Christ Jesus, because through Christ Jesus the law of the Spirit who gives life has set you free from the law of sin and death. For what the law was powerless to do because it was weakened by the flesh, God did by sending His own Son in the likeness of sinful flesh to be a sin offering. And so He condemned sin in the flesh.

I first met Constance Cooper in the fall of 2009 in her role as my cosmetologist. She was attending a local church in Antioch, California, where she was a member of the choir and praise team. She attended Bible Study and Sunday School regularly. Although I have known Connie for a short time, I am impressed by her love for God. Anytime you visit her shop, you will find her testifying, witnessing, quoting Scripture or sharing the goodness of our God.

She has continued to be open and candid about her life experiences prior to giving her life completely to the Lord. Matthews 26:41 says, Keep watching and praying that you many not enter into temptation; the Spirit is willing, but the flesh is weak. She consistently talked about her proclivity for helping others and giving back to the community. In my opinion, she has successfully accomplished this with the writing of her book "The Chronicles of Connie." Connie has lived a hard life. However, she maintains a somewhat naïve attitude towards trusting people. She loves hard and hurts easily, which is unique in that most of those who have been hurt often find it hard to love.

The spectrum of substance abuse has four phases, which are experimental use; recreational use; abuse and addiction. Drug use is deceptive because no one sees when one phase begins and another one ends as the lines are blurred. Along with drug use comes every other fleshly device. Connie does a good job of making this case. Her book takes the glamour and eventually the fun out of substance use and I hope that young people will, after reading her book, walk away with this notion.

Veronica Baines, LCSW

Owner, Life Transitions

~ *Foreword* ~

How great and awesome is our God; For He has done marvelous things in the life of His daughter, Minister Constance Cooper, who once was lost but now is found; was blind but now she sees.

As I read the book "The Chronicles of Connie," by Constance Cooper, I couldn't help but reflect on the woman with the issue of blood. How this woman went through the motions of life but she never lived. She was just going through the movements of life; with no one really seeing her. No one knew her pain, no one really knew her struggle. As I read the book, the first thing I see in Connie is her big smile, a smile so alluring that it covered her pain; a smile so captivating that you couldn't see her brokenness, nor will you see her inner loneliness. And so she dwells behind the smile like the woman with the issue of blood. I could see her now moving through the crowds; the crowds of people that represented the shadows of her life. This woman suffered, this woman was confused, and this woman was alone; over-powered by the shadows that followed her in and out of her pain.

I am sure she lived a life of many wrong decisions; I am sure she turned to those that continued to lead her down a wrong and twisted painful course; for none of them could really comfort her, none of them could really help her. For her needs were far greater than her friends could see. And so she armed herself with her smile—the only shield she had. And she continued her journey through the shadows of so many people, until one day she decided to no longer live among the shadows. She decided it was time; it was time to truly come from among all the shadows of life, those familiar shadows, and the shadows that were awaiting her.

And so, this woman hidden in her pit, shadowed by her smile; driven by the desire to become someone that she always wanted to be, but not knowing how to be, decided to take a tremendous step of Faith and stepped into her Heavenly Father's Arms, and give herself to Him completely and totally. So she mustered up all her strength, a strength that comes from the desperate parts of her soul and she pushed her way pass the familiar faces, pass the broken promises, pass her loneliness and reached out and touched the hem of His garment. For she knew that God had her healing, God had her hope, He had her promise waiting for her. The promise of life; the promise of prosperity.

You did it Connie! You were that woman; those shadows were the pain, the frustration, the drugs, the dark lifestyles, the anger, the countless tears, and yes, even at times yourself. But Connie, you never gave up on yourself and you never gave up on God. You became naked before God, so that He may heal you. You trusted God and you revealed yourself to others that they may have hope, the kind of hope that surpasses all understanding. You shared with them your story. You became vulnerable and yet stood strong as you opened up to the world so that finally they would see beyond your smile. You allowed them to step into your pain; walk around your struggle, and yes, even feel your shame. But out of all you shared, out of all you gave, the most important thing was that you shared with them Christ and the hope, power, and victory that comes from knowing Him.

"The Chronicles of Connie" are real; there are times you want to cry as you read through the pages of her struggle. There are times you will sit in disbelief as she tells her story, but as you read through the pages there is one thing for sure, you're sure to meet Jesus who was her guiding light. You're sure to meet Jesus who is all powerful. You're sure to meet Jesus who surely saved her life.

In "The Chronicles of Connie" you'll meet a little girl who lost her childhood but was allowed to be a babe in Christ Jesus. You'll read of a young girl who was pushed into a lifestyle that no young girl should ever have to experience, and yet you see her rise victorious in the midst of it all. And you'll meet a woman who hemorrhages from the depth of her spirit but was healed completely by Christ our Saviour. As you read "The Chronicles of Connie" you will wonder why on earth isn't she dead, sleeping in her grave. But then you will feel the spirit of God saying, "Because I promised her that I would never leave her nor forsake her.

MY Daughter in Christ Jesus, I am so pleased with you...You did it! Now keep on seeking God for the increase, for your journey has just begun.

Pastor Phyllis Scott,

Pastor, Tree of Life Empowerment Ministries

and

Founder of Exodus Program,

A rescue center for sexually exploited

teens and women.

~ Introduction ~

In this introduction to my autobiography I would first like to give all Honor and Praise to my Lord and Savior Jesus Christ who is the head of my life. I have so many things to be grateful for. In God's Holy word it says what the devil meant for bad God would turn it around to bless you with. Truth be told I should be totally ashamed and embarrassed, but I'm not. God blessed me to stay here on this earth, His earth. The bible says the earth is the Lord's and the fullness thereof. *The earth is the LORD's, and everything in it, the world, and all who live in it;* --Psalms 24:1. So if God allows circumstances in our lives, we should rejoice in all things. *And you and the Levites and the aliens among you shall rejoice in all the good things the LORD your God has given to you and your household* -- Deuteronomy 26:11. *Be joyful always;* --1Thessalonians 5:16. He says all things work together for the good of them that love Him who are called according to His purpose. Which meant to me everything that I went through in my past was for my good and for His Glory. *And we know that in all things God works for the good of those who love him, who have been called according to his purpose* --Romans 8:28.

1

If you are insulted because of the name of Christ, you are blessed, for the Spirit of glory and of God rests on you - -1Peter 4:14.

As I sit here and I type out this book early this beautiful morning I realize that my steps had already been ordered by the Lord. *If the LORD delights in a man's way, he makes his steps firm;* --Psalms 37:23. So when they say don't do drugs please take heed all my young teenagers, and young adults. If you haven't started, don't and if you have, please stop now before you get to a point that only God can save you from.

I'm sure those of us who have had the privilege to come to know Jesus as our Lord and Savior and stopped using drugs, if not for the grace of God, we would not be here to tell our story. We also know that the first time is never the last. So as I said before, please do not start at all using drugs, please.

There are so many other things that go hand in hand with addiction. There are spirits. These spirits are loneliness, guilt, failure, and fear and anxiety. There are more spirits that come along with addiction. We'll just start with those to name a few. When you start to slack off, missing work, start missing appointments, you don't come home, you stay out all night long, you forget about the kids, your home, and your family, husband, and wife (if you have one), face it you are addicted.

It is never fun being addicted! Addiction covers all color lines. It covers all financial brackets. Addiction has no racism. It doesn't care whose lives it destroys, whose home it tears apart, whose job is lost, the reputation it destroys or character it tarnishes.

I will give you a taste of my journey down a long, dark, lonely road that led me back to Jesus. Go with me. Let me show how God can take your mess and make it a message. He can take your tragedies and make them triumphs. He can take your test and make it your testimony. He gave me the victory over all my downfalls. Every wrong move, He made it right. I love the Lord. He never turned His back on me. He loved me in spite of me. This is to let that one person know who thinks that life is too hard, that they can't make it, to keep on pushing forward, never look back. Always look to a hill. That is where your help comes from.

My life represents a struggle with myself. Most people like to play the blame game. I personally know different. It was no one else's fault but my own. I decided to keep on getting high and not ask for help until it was too late, after too much time. None of us are perfect, but with God all things are possible.

This book is for every woman, man, or even a child, who thinks their life is over. It's not. Never give up never give in. Always trust that God is fully aware of your situation and all He is waiting on is for you to ask for help.

You are not the only one in that situation, someone else is always worse off than you. Remember the race is not given to the swift, but to the one who endures to the end. So don't you give up sister, brother, stay on the battlefield! I seriously suggest if you're not saved and you don't know the Lord as your personal Savior then you should get to know Him for yourself, accept Him in your heart. He's waiting for you. He loves you Amen.

Here is the Sinner's Prayer for you if you haven't accepted Jesus as Lord of your life. Now you can. It's very simple just repeat these words and be transformed in an instant:

Father it is written in Your Word that if we confess with our mouth and I believe in my heart that God raised Jesus from the dead and He is Lord, I shall be saved. Therefore, Father I confess that Jesus is my Lord. I make Him Lord of my life right now. I believe in my heart that God raised Jesus from dead. I renounce my past life with satan and close the door to any of his devices. I thank You for forgiving me of all my sins. Jesus is my Lord, and I am a

new creature, old things have passed away and all things
are become new in Jesus name. Amen.

That's it. If you said this prayer and you truly believe
all it says then you are saved. Welcome to the Kingdom,
we love you in Jesus name. Amen.

~ *Chapter 1* ~

I remember the first time I ever tried drugs – I was about fifteen years old. I met some young girls who stayed next door to my father. I had just moved in after my parents got a divorce. I can remember my very first sip of beer. I was about five or six years old. I would even take puffs off my parent's cigarettes. I guess by now you have to be saying to yourself, this child was out of control and you are correct in saying that. I was a spoiled kid.

My mother and father had me in the seventies. My father was fifty, and my mom was thirty, they were twenty years apart. My Father took bets on horses for a living (you would call him a bookie) and my mother was a cocktail waitress, and they always had late night parties. My mother had four friends who I called my aunties. They would come over all the time after my mom would get off work late nights. I really didn't see too much at least not until I was older in my teens. My mom used to always have friends come over late after work and they would party into the early morning. Not all the time but most of the time. Let me make it clear that they only came over on the weekends. So when they did they would have me dance. I could dance really good as a child. So lets say I was and always have

7

been the life of the party. I would pour drinks, light cigarettes, play records and I did everything. I was quite the little cocktail waitress.

This is how dysfunction starts in the family. Never under any circumstance let your children see you doing grown up things that they shouldn't. They want to be just like us because they look up to us. We are the first role models, and their minds are just like sponges. What it soaks up depends on you.

Well back to my story. At those late night parties is where I started sneaking in sips of beer more often. I know I'm not the only one who had that kind of family in the hood. You just become a product of your environment. So as years passed I remember the very first time I actually saw cocaine. My mother had a friend named Carolan. We went to her house for a Christmas party and I will never forget it. Her friend passed around an album cover with a white substance on it. As they passed it around they sniffed the powder up their noses with red and white straws. It was crazy. My mom put my head under a jacket as she tried it. I don't believe she really liked that stuff though because I never saw or heard of her doing it again. At least a few years would go by before I would ever see that stuff again.

When I was about eight years old, I saw it a second time. Then around the age of ten is when I saw cocaine for the third time. There was a documentary about drug abuse which showed the horrors of how years of using cocaine could eat away your nose. The results of its use could cause the loss of your family, your home, or your job. It would be a disaster for anyone to use drugs period. Now I guess you would ask why would anyone use drugs after seeing that? Well let me explain it to you. You know how they say don't get close to the fire or you will get burned. Well that's how it was with drugs. I knew they were bad but everybody I knew was getting high. They were getting high on something whether it was weed, or alcohol. They smoked cigarettes, and some of them did the stronger drugs too.

I can honestly say that after seeing the documentary it scared me but it also made me just a little bit more curious about drugs. I believe the reason why it made me more curious, was because it glamorized drugs in the beginning of the program. It showed people in the eighteenth century, doing drugs and having fun. The had drugs in their rings, in lockets, they put it in drinks and in cigarettes; they just out right partied real hard with drugs. So to me, it looked fun at first. But there was something else the program showed that changed my life. It also made me curious about sex. Yeah that's right, it strongly influenced me to want to experience sex. So if you didn't hear me before, watch what your kids are looking at on T.V.

Now what I want you to realize is that this documentary was about two, maybe three hours long. It was in segments, so it started with the fun and the sex and how they used drugs in soda, medicine and alcohol. Then in the next segment it showed how families started to suffer from their addictions, and how the medicines that was supposed to help started to become addictive to the user. Drugs weren't helping, they were making matters worse. People were sick, they looked like dope fiends. Even their children were sick from addiction.

As the program progressed it moved into the 60s era. Now in the 60s drugs became more and more popular again. The documentary showed people partying, having orgies and how it appeared fun to use drugs. At least it seemed to me at the time while watching it on television. Then the next segment showed the tragedy of drug use. People were now in rehabs, on the streets after loosing homes, cars and their children because of drugs. What caught my attention the most was when it showed this woman and man with both their noses eaten away totally from snorting cocaine. Even though I remembered seeing that and the people in the rehabs, it didn't scare me enough for me to not want to try them.

I don't care what anyone says, but when I saw my mother getting high I believe that was why I always wanted to do drugs. So be careful what you take your kids around or even what they see on the T.V. Believe me they are always watching. Even when you think they aren't, they are. We are the role models. I also believe it was a well-laid plan or should I say trick of the devil to try to kill me ahead of time. Although God allowed it, He always had a plan for my life. *For I know the plans I have for you," declares the LORD, "plans to prosper you and not to harm you, plans to give you hope and a future* --Jeremiah 29:11. But when we confess Him as Lord of our lives, He comes in and sets everything in order. *That if you confess with your mouth, "Jesus is Lord," and believe in your heart that God raised him from the dead, you will be saved* --Romans 10:9. *If anyone acknowledges that Jesus is the Son of God, God lives in him and he in God* --1John 4:15. *But thanks be to God, who always leads us in triumphal procession in Christ and through us spreads everywhere the fragrance of the knowledge of him* --2Corinthians 2:14. Thank you

Jesus! Years later my mom and dad divorced. That's when my life really took a turn for the worse.

~ *Chapter 2* ~

When my father moved out we stayed with my mother at first. She was a good mother and we never wanted for anything. She really believed and still does believe in taking care of her family, especially her kids. Without question when they got a divorce, it was hard for all of us. When I say all of us, I mean my sisters. We loved both my father and mother. It was a dramatic change for our lives. We had dreams and we thought our family would always be together.

My sister Tina was the first to move in with my father, even though he wasn't her natural dad. My father was a good man and stepfather. He never made any difference between my sisters and me. He took care of all of us the same, no difference. When my sister Tina went to college, she had my nephew Isaiah. It was my dad and moms first grandchild. Even though it was supposed to be a happy occasion it wasn't. My mom had kicked my sister out and that's how she ended up at my dad's. She had nowhere else to go because her natural mom was suffering from addiction at that time. I also believe my mother was suffering from addiction too. Now that I look back, there were too many unstable behavior patterns.

Let's get back to my story. I'll let her tell hers if she wants to write her own book. The next time I saw drugs was after my sister Fleta moved out to live with my dad too because she was a lesbian. My mother went off on my sister because my mother didn't understand why she was a lesbian. She beat her and told her to get out. Now when I look back she must have been out of her mind. She thought she could beat the lesbianism out of my sister. Crazy right?

Now here we are, my mom and me--just the two of us living in the house together. Talk about fun at first, but after a while it all hit the fan. She started having all sorts of strange men coming over and spending the night. Men I had seen before and some I hadn't. It was off the hook. I thought to myself that she was just waiting for my father to leave, or maybe she was really unhappy?

There was one man in particular I really remember. His name was Rudy and he was a child molester. The reason why I say that is because he used to always chase me around the house and pin me down and say he was going to steal my stuff. He didn't use those nice words at all. He was quite the potty mouth. My mom always left me with this man because she worked at night and stayed in the bed half the day. Remember, she was a cocktail waitress. While working half the night away she took care of me and that man during the day.

Anyway this man was heavily on drugs--heavily. He smoked a lot of weed and was also a heroin addict. When my father found out about him living with us, he went off. I remember when my dad came over. My mom wasn't there so dad took me with him. My father already knew Rudy who was known for being down at a local hotel hangout. Dad told him to tell Shirley "I got my baby," and to call him when she got home.

I have to backup a little because I'm getting ahead of myself. I also saw Rudy snorting cocaine. I remember when I walked up on him, I said "yuck, you're doing drugs." He said, "Your mom does it too." That's when I peeked around the corner and I saw her snorting. My heart was broken and I didn't want my mother to be on drugs, but she was.

So fast forward to when I got picked up by my dad. My mom came to my dad's and that was when I said I wanted to stay with him. You see Rudy had been staying with us for at least six or seven months. So by the time my dad came over, I had already told him I wanted to leave there. I lost friends because Rudy played with them the same way he played with me. Let's make this clear, that wasn't playing, but I thought it was. My friends told their parents so they couldn't come over to my house ever again. Also when I was alone with him he let me smoke weed and drink with him. Can you believe it? I was only twelve years old, maybe thirteen. Anyway, being around Rudy was the beginning of the spiral down effect of my life.

I changed from being innocent to being sneaky and a thief. I went from a kid who use to like riding my bike to one who wanted to sit in the house with a grown man and smoke weed, cigarettes, drink alcohol and get more curious about heavier drugs.

I admit the devil had a plan to kill me a long time before I was even sixteen. He knew God had a plan for my life and he wanted to stop it before it actually took flight. Thank God He's the God of second, third, and fourth chances.

I can't stress it enough. Always check out what your kids are doing and who they're hanging out with. Please, please check out the people you hang out with too. You never know what could be happening with them and your kids.

Before I go any further, I will say I never had sex with that man but I had plenty of opportunity to. Rudy would chase me around the house like we were kids. He was a real nut case. He played with me in a sexual way making sexual passes at me, and he even tried to stick his hands in my pants. I must have been really strong because he didn't scare me at first. Not only was he having sex with my mother but he wanted to have sex with me too.

I remember one day he went too far. He tried to stick his finger in my, well you know what I'm trying to say. That's the day when I saw him doing cocaine. To me he was fun as long as he was smoking weed, but when he hit that coke he was someone different, totally different.

Let me tell you how he got in the house in the first place. He was the victim of a stabbing. Now when I look back, I believe it had to be drug related. Anyway, my mom felt sorry for him, so she took him in. He didn't have anywhere to go so my mom figured she would take care of him. He had no family and not very many friends, at least that's what my mom said. Anyway, that's when her mood swings started. I remember her having a personal stash. She had a straw on her dresser in a little container. When I think back, I can see how it would make a little girl curious. We look up to our mothers because we love and respect them. When I asked her about the package that's when she told me to stay out of her room. But this was my favorite room, outside of the bathroom. Let me explain. My mom had so much stuff, like jewelry, perfume, shoes, purses, I mean she had everything a little girl could ever want to play with in her room. Then there was the bathroom. In there was an overflow of makeup, more perfume, bubble bath, eyelashes--I mean my mom had everything. She was the bomb!

After a while it all went down hill for us, and I realized I needed some sense of normalcy, so that's when I decided that I wanted to live with my father.

Flash back to when my father came to the house. He actually came to move me out, so that was the reason for him coming over. When I spent the night, I told him I didn't want to go back home, I wanted to stay with him. I told him everything about the man who was staying at my mom's house.

Naturally my father was extremely upset with my mother, and wanted to do some harm to that man. So instead of hurting my mother and Rudy, he decided to just tell her I was staying there with him and for her to do something about that man before he does! I thank God for having my father here on earth do something quick because there is no telling what my life would be like if I hadn't gotten out of there. He also told my mother that if that Negro wasn't out of the house by the end of the day, he would kill her and him. Of course he didn't mean it but he wanted that dope fiend out of the house, immediately! And he had his .45 in the car as well when he came to pick me up.

My father was really old school and since he was twenty years older than my mom, when he meant business, he meant business. My mom really meant well herself but she just still had a lot of partying in her. I believe she was old school in a lot of ways too. She believed in marriage and had two previous marriages to prove it. Thank God for His divine intervention, but my struggles were far from over.

~ *Chapter 3* ~

The move was as successful as it could possibly be, considering the circumstances. There were all three sisters staying with my father in a two-bedroom house on the other side of town. My father was a Southern man born in 1920, in Gilmer, Texas, the deep South. He had old school ways and accomplished so much during his lifetime. He helped to lay the first asphalt in Dallas, Texas; was one of many to help with the Alaskan pipeline; and owned several restaurants in Southern California. In addition he owned and operated a vending machine company. He had the kind of machines that played music as well as the ones that sold candy and soda pop. He did all that with a sixth grade education. Even though he lost some if not most of his businesses, he still had an entrepreneurial spirit. Whatever he started, he finished.

When he and my mother met, they really hit it off. He was still an attractive, mature, older man, and my mother was an extremely attractive young woman. They had lots of fun in the beginning and they really hit off so much that I came out of that relationship. My father had been raising my sisters with my mother before I was born, for at least a year or two, and their bond was so tight. That's the reason why my sisters moved in with my dad when they left my mom's house. To them he was their father. There was never any difference between any of us as far as he was concerned; he didn't love me nor anyone of my sisters more than the other. We were all equal in his eyes.

My father was and still is very special to me. I will always love my father even though he has gone on to be with the Lord. Love you daddy. I just wanted to paint a picture for you of the relationship we all shared with my mom and dad.

Moving forward. My father was a bookie in his later years. Did I know it was illegal? No, not until I was old enough to understand what that word even meant. He ran a gambling shack where they played craps, bet on the horses, basketball games, football, and played music. My mom took me there to stay only when she was running errands and if no one else was able to keep me. I wasn't put in any danger at any time. Everybody there was good at keeping me out of danger. I had plenty of "uncles" who were my father's friends and customers. They always gave me money, so I had lots of pennies, one-dollar bills, and all kinds of change. I'm painting a picture for you of who this man was and why he tolerated so much. He was truly old school.

Fast-forward. While growing up, we all knew the difference between right and wrong, even though we were raised in this static environment. We knew to respect ourselves, so we would respect our parents, our elders, aunts, uncles, our neighbors, our teachers, and our friends as well as our enemies. You have to give what you want to receive, Amen. We were raised going to church with my grandmother and our aunts. So we had the principles to a proper upbringing as children.

We knew not to talk back or even try to roll our eyes, like little girls do sometimes nowadays. We also knew that if we thought about talking back, it was whipping time. No foul language or anything like that was tolerated because we knew how to behave ourselves.

Now back to the move. My father had this idea that if you wanted to smoke, you had to do it in the house. He said if you smoked outside you would stand a good chance at getting the wrong thing or even worse, you could probably get some bad weed. They might give you some sherm, which is a hallucinogenic, meaning you could get high and never come back down from it. Most people who smoke that stuff usually are never the same any more.

When I was fourteen years old my father said that if all my schoolwork and household chores were done, I could smoke on the weekends. At first it was cool, because I was making good grades, passing at least. Then on the weekends I would finish all my chores, go outside for a little while and then around three o'clock I'd come in the house and smoke until I had the munchies. I ate and then smoked some more. Now I know that sounds crazy, but my father was an old man, so he thought it just might work out, and it did at first.

I know my father meant well, we just didn't know it was wrong. It seemed so right, because that's all we knew at that time. I believe my father wanted to protect us so boys wouldn't disrespect us out in the world. They wouldn't try to take advantage and say we were easy. There were times when we would have a beer or a wine cooler and a box full of weed that he would break out with us on the weekends. Yeah, he hid it from us during the week so we couldn't be tempted or lose focus.

So on Friday, if all our work was done, it was on, it was party time. Before I go any further I have to mention my Uncle Ted. He was the one who stayed with my father before me and my sisters moved in. Initially, it was me, my dad and Uncle Ted and my sisters didn't come until later. Uncle Ted was a World War II veteran, and was also a great man who taught me how to cook, to bake cakes, wash dishes and everything. I miss him still, love you Uncle Ted, always.

Now back to the fun house. We couldn't smoke outside or even on the front porch. My father said that we should be ladies and do our business in the house, not where everyone could see us. Have respect for ourselves. After about two months my oldest sister Tina moved in with us. She had just had my nephew Isaiah, so at first I had the room to myself, but my oldest sister got it because she needed it. Remember I was still a child, she was a grown woman and she needed privacy, at least that's what my father said. Then after about a year she moved into her own apartment in Vallejo.

Fleta was another story all together. Since she wasn't home much, I had the room to myself again and I did a lot of changing during the process. Fleta had so much going on. She was changing and coming into who she was to become. She took her first girlfriend to the prom. Yeah you heard me right. With her first girlfriend, is how I saw my sister first do cocaine. She was the person I saw up close actually doing drugs. At first it didn't seem troublesome, but drugs became a distraction to her and her education. And as she started to get high more frequently, cutting school increased.

Fleta and her girlfriend were doing anything and everything to get what they wanted. That's what made me upset about the partying. It was like the sister I used to look up to just didn't have time for me anymore. Then the neighbors started to hang out more. They were like sharks, always had their hands out, but they were the only friends I had. At least that's what it felt like to me. My friends had a lot of cousins, I mean cousins! They really did all kinds of stuff. I mean everything like crack, weed, alcohol, sex and prostitution.

That's just like the devil, come in and get the youth early. Teenagers, little kids, he doesn't care, he just wants your soul and your blessings. I had no idea that my sister knew the neighbors because she was never at home when I was there. My father told me to stay away from them. Funny he would let me smoke weed and stuff but I couldn't hang out with the neighbors. He knew what they were doing. I on the other hand was still green. My sister was already turned out, so when she came home one time she and her girlfriend were kissing in front of me and doing drugs too. It was wild. They would do all kinds of stuff. Use your imagination.

One time in particular she had been gone all weekend, so when she came in she started snorting right in front of me. She told me I couldn't handle what she was doing, but maybe one day when I grew up. She didn't let me do it with her at all, not one time. By now I was running from this drug. Yeah cocaine was everywhere I went and I was determined at first to not let this drug get a hold of me. But unfortunately curiosity got the best of me.

My sister partied with the neighbor girls as well. There was one girl who had the block sown up when it came to dope. She sold everything and she had the girls next door working for her. I didn't know that my sister had gone to junior high school with the "queen pin" as I liked to call her. My father also knew that my sister was hanging out with these girls, but since she was older it was OK for her, at least that's what we thought.

My sister was eighteen and I was going on fourteen, and things had gotten out of hand pretty quick. My sister was doing too much by then. She and her girlfriend were having sexual relations while I was in the same room. We shared the bedroom, so when they thought I was asleep they would get busy. But Fleta eventually moved out. She didn't just move out she moved all the way to Chicago, with some friends she grew up with. She started going to cosmetology school out there as well. After she left I started to hang out with the neighbor girls. They lived in

San Francisco, but came out to stay with their grandmother in the neighborhood on the weekends. There were two sisters and a cousin. Their uncle who took care of them rode a motorcycle and belonged to a motorcycle club in Richmond. I had a lot going on at a young age, didn't I?

As I mentioned before, drugs were everywhere. I got a chance to go out to their house a few times. One time in particular, the two sisters had run away but the cousin was still living with her father, the uncle. While I was spending the weekend with the cousin, her father gave her a package. Well you can guess what was in it. Yeah, that man gave his daughter cocaine. Now what kind of man would give his daughter drugs? A butthole--not a real father. Well, you know what happened next. I did cocaine for the first time at the age of fourteen. Who would think that someone at that age would be thinking of getting high. Not even me. I really thought I would be able to resist the devil. I didn't have that much strength to withstand him back then, because I had stopped walking with God for a time.

I remember being in San Francisco and her father coming home that night with her stepmom. He handed his daughter this package of white substance and she put some of it in cigarettes and we smoked it. I didn't know what to feel but I do know it took me hours to fall asleep.

You might be asking yourself how old was this young lady? She was a lot older than me. She had to be at least sixteen or seventeen years old. My father didn't think she was as bad as her cousins, but little did he know she was just the same as they were when it came to drugs.

So that night I smoked cocaine for the first time and we did four cigarettes and I thought I didn't feel anything, but I did. I couldn't sleep. That would be the first but not my last time with that drug. I know it's crazy but we considered that to be fun.

A few months later my sister came home with a white girl, and this big golden retriever. Yes a big golden dog. Talk about tripping. We got high a lot. I started going to the gay bars with her and the girlfriend all the time. I was about sixteen then and I had fake I.D. By now there were always drugs around.

I truly believe that my addiction was a generational curse. You know in the Word it says the sins of the parents will visit the children to the third and fourth generation. *The LORD's curse is on the house of the wicked, but he blesses the home of the righteous* --Proverbs 3:33. I believe that! It's my Fathers Word! Whatever the case, drugs really messes up a person's life. When my sister returned to

Chicago, I was left alone with no supervision and a drug addiction that I didn't realize I had until years later.

~ *Chapter 4* ~

Now I will fast forward a few years. My father fell in love with a woman who just happened to be the aunt of the girls next door. This woman was a devil in disguise and she was never who she said she was. She was a wicked evil stepmother just like in the Cinderella story. My father was lonely and she was greedy. The girls next door lived with their grandmother who was delusional. She had been burned in a fire and she would say some of the craziest things, like she was still on fire, so they would sprinkle baby powder on her to cool her off. That is part of the reason there was always so much stuff going on, because Ms. Louise didn't have much control over her house anyway. She couldn't. She was partially paralyzed in her mind, and she was also psychotic. So when the children were left there they just ran wild.

Now the woman who my father fell in love with had three children of her own. I went to school with one of them, her son, who just happened to be in love with me in junior high school. After my dad and his mom got together nothing was happening, because we were brother and sister now. Anyway, my father took this woman in and she came in and took over the house. At first it seemed like it would work out but soon after it didn't. She started to change and she became more and more selfish. Not to mention, her sons sold crack cocaine for a living and all she and her daughter did was sit back and collect the cash. They were lazy, and just plain selfish.

Her daughter also had a daughter, which made her a grandmother. I will leave my fathers' romance out of this story. Eventually I started to watch my two stepbrothers cook up dope. They snorted dope, as they cooked up the dope. Their mother had all these friends that would get high too. I never saw her touch the stuff herself but her friends got high for sure. Then the rest of the family was all on dope. I mean from the top to the bottom. She had two siblings that were hooked on heroin, the uncle was a coke head, and the other sister was a pill head, who from time to time would snort dope too. So now you understand I have always been around people who were on dope. The only people who weren't on drugs were on my mother's side of the family. My aunts all had jobs, careers, some were in the military, and others went to college. Mostly all of them had some form of extended education, but I had one uncle who had a drug problem and still does to this day.

So back to my story. We looked like a happy family from the outside but that was far from the truth. Not only were these people users but they were very deceitful. They used my father up. The oldest son was a crack head. He stole from us, stole dope from his own brother, and money from his mother, sister and even me. Even though he was a crack head he would still hustle with his brother in the day time and when they would come in from being out all day they would go to the "Back Track." That was the hang out at night and my father's work area during the day. So they would sit back there and get high and kick it hard all night.

The youngest son always protected me from anyone and anything. It didn't matter who it was and what was going on, he had my back. I remember when his brother stole money from me, he replaced it right away. That's because he was different from his family. He wasn't selfish or stingy but was a very giving person. Eventually the older brother had to go. His habit was so bad it was affecting my father's and their mother's relationship. His mother would always let him back in the house, but my father wasn't having it. So that's when they decided to move out. She said it wasn't working but the police were watching the house anyway and that was too risky for my father. Plus they were down right ghetto. They had good taste in furniture, clothes, and hair but just tacky people. After all that, we were also told that the police were going to raid our house for drugs. Can you imagine? Now when they left, they left us in the house with no furniture, no curtains, they did us bad.

That devastated my father, because he really loved her. She decided to leave because she loved her son so much more, that she was willing to go if he couldn't stay. She left us like a welfare case. That woman was a piece of work. Plus my father's business wasn't doing too well anyway, not to mention he was in debt.

Now we are by ourselves, and the sons managed to turn our block into a twenty four hour dope street before they left. You see how quickly the enemy can come in and turn your life upside down and he will work through anyone, anything, anywhere. *The thief comes only to steal and kill and destroy; I have come that they may have life, and have it to the full* --John 10:10. Always be fully armored with the Word of God. *Take the helmet of salvation and the sword of the Spirit, which is the word of God* --Ephesians 6:17. *For the word of God is living and active. Sharper than any double-edged sword, it penetrates even to dividing soul and spirit, joints and marrow; it judges the thoughts and attitudes of the heart* --Hebrews 4:12. You can see how the neighborhood went bad quickly.

I started hanging out with the girls next door, because they had run away from San Francisco to grandmother's house where they were selling drugs out of it and dating these big time drug dealers. They thought they had it made but they were about to be lost and turned out before they knew it.

So as time went on, I started to smoke more weed and get drunk with the girls. We dated some of the same men, and were out of control. It still took me a long time to snort cocaine because I was afraid that my dad would find out. So when I was around the corner at the queen pin's house where the girls worked out of too, I would just kick it, drink, and smoke weed. Remember I said they worked for the queen pin. They were her runners. I said no to snorting, until I couldn't say no anymore. Peer pressure finally got me. I don't remember when I first snorted coke, but once I started I didn't stop. I believe the one reason my father never noticed I was high, was because I stayed up all night anyway. I had always stayed up late watching television since I was a small child. So for me to be staying up late all night wasn't hard. As for my personality, I wasn't different to my family. So once I started, I started everything. Yeah, they turned me out for real.

Let me take you back to when I was in junior high school before I started my downward spiral. One day I decided I was going to take some weed to school, but three girls thought they were going to punk me. They stayed around the corner from my mom's and they also hung out around the corner from my father's house. When they asked to see my stuff, I let them and they wouldn't give it back to me. Now the first time I gave them a pass, so I let them keep it. But when two of them tried to punk me again I said no. They followed me home and then I let them have it. They thought they were going to punk me again but it didn't work out like that. I took them on and beat both of them.

So you see, I had enemy forces after me for a long time but to God be the glory. He always had angels watching over me. I want you to see the pattern developing. The enemy will always try to keep you from your purpose, but God has already worked it out for your good. *No temptation has seized you except what is common to man. And God is faithful; he will not let you be tempted beyond what you can bear. But when you are tempted, he will also provide a way out so that you can stand up under it* --1Corinthians 10:13.

Remember you have a testimony, it is your past and if you've been delivered of anything then it's rich and it's for someone else who might need to be encouraged.

Fast forward. Now I have completely dropped out of school. I was having sex, looking at porno, drinking, and snorting coke. There was an old pervert who stayed next door who used to ask me to sleep with him for a couple of bucks. He wasn't the first and definitely wasn't last. I started buying my own coke. I would watch porno and get high all by myself. I would lock my door and play my music really loud. Talk about a 180. I went from going to school, trying to be dancer, as normal as I could be, to being a 16-year-old drug and sex addict who was lost and turned out.

If you're a young girl reading this book or you have a teen family member, pay attention to everything they do and check their rooms and their friends. You never know what they might have hidden in their closets.

~ *Chapter 5* ~

I started making runs for my father, who at the time was a bookie. Now we have furniture in the house and I worked every morning for him making forty dollars a day. That was how I supported my habit. I was working for my dad and dating old men. That's what we call turning tricks. When I was sixteen was the very first time I had ever gotten pregnant. I called myself being slick by trying to move back in with my mom. She stayed in Pinole at the time, and she had no idea I was pregnant until one day she noticed that I kept throwing up. She said, "you must be pregnant but you aren't getting rid of it." At first I was all gung ho about it but then reality set in. I wasn't ready to have a baby yet. My father wasn't on to anything and I thought I would just go run and hide from him, but it didn't happen that way.

When my mom told my dad about it there was a huge fight about me keeping or aborting my baby. My mom wanted me to keep the child because she was already talking about a welfare check but my dad was worried about my future. She said we would go down to the welfare office and get food stamps, Section 8 and everything. So since my father knew my mom better than I did he told her to bring me home so we could talk about it.

Needless to say my father talked me into having my first, but definitely not my last abortion. At first it seemed like my problem was solved, but about six months later I was pregnant again with my oldest child.

My life had so many different ups and downs, that just writing down these few years of memories has made me thankful for everything that the Lord has brought me from. He kept me in the midst of madness. He saved me in spite of myself. There were so many things that should have killed me, but God. *If we confess our sins, he is faithful and just and will forgive us our sins and purify us from all unrighteousness* --1John 1:9. God has a purpose for your life if you just wait on Him and trust and believe He will make a way. *Trust in the LORD with all your heart and lean not on your own understanding; v6. in all your ways acknowledge him, and he will make your paths straight* -- Proverbs 3:5-6. He has purpose for my life and yours too.

~ *Chapter 6* ~

Six months later, I am pregnant and decide to keep who was to be my oldest son Eric. Let me slow down because this book is about my addiction and my struggle to stay clean and alive. All the while, God had His hand all over my life. *In righteousness you will be established: Tyranny will be far from you; you will have nothing to fear. Terror will be far removed; it will not come near you* --Isaiah 54:14. *As for God, his way is perfect; the word of the LORD is flawless. He is a shield for all who take refuge in him* --Psalms 18:30. So even though I didn't snort coke while I was pregnant with my son I started to sell weed. It was this dirt weed we used to call booda tie, or chocolate tie. I started to smoke weed too. I stayed nauseated all the time so it helped my stomach. As far as the baby was concerned I never got into any trouble at the doctors office. I did it for three months, but I slowed down after the third month. So I kept weed around all the time.

I was in love with my oldest son's father. He was tall, dark and handsome. And yes, he was a drug dealer too. It seemed like everybody in my life was doing something illegal. I always attracted some of the most unlikely characters. It seemed like my life was going nowhere and fast too.

I can remember stealing my dad's car and driving to Oakland. I was chasing my son's father around. He used to hide from me all the time, and was trying to deny that my son was his child. Of course this was his child. Then he didn't love me as much as I loved him, if he loved me at all. He didn't have his own house either. If I would be standing outside, he would leave me with his brother on the dope track while he was running away from me or making dope runs. His brother was dating my play sister; I say that because she was my dad's lady friend's daughter. I was so blind, I would be waiting outside and he would never come to see me or anything, and I was carrying his child.

This is one book that I know will help young girls and do them some good. Just because he says he loves you doesn't mean he will treat you with love and respect. Love is an action, not just a word. *And so we know and rely on the love God has for us. God is love. Whoever lives in love lives in God, and God in him* --1John 4:16. God shows us He loves us every day, because we can see, hear, walk, talk, and we can breathe on our own. *Praise be to the Lord, to God our Savior, who daily bears our burdens. Selah* -- Psalms 68:19. *The Lord is good to all; he has compassion on all he has made* -- Psalms 145:9.

Somebody woke up this morning and couldn't breathe on their own. Somebody woke up and couldn't walk on they're own, so we should always be thankful for the life we do have. *But in your great mercy you did not put an end to them or abandon them, for you are a gracious and merciful God* --Nehemiah 9:31. *I will sing of the LORD's great love forever; with my mouth I will make your faithfulness known through all generations* --Psalms 89:1. Somebody didn't wake up at all. Amen. That's another story, so let's move forward.

So here I am, about to deliver my son Eric, and I couldn't have him vaginally because of complications. I had toxemia, which is high blood pressure during pregnancy. I loved my baby so much that I was able to stay sober for the last six months of my pregnancy. And then it happened. I hooked up with my friend who had the ultimate trick. He had money and he loved to get high. Of course this was a catch. He wanted to see two girls together. Talking about a big jump, that was the first time that I had ever done anything like that. Needless to say we stayed out all night. We bought cocaine and he had alcohol. Thank God for Jesus, because I'm still alive today to even tell this story. *Christ redeemed us from the curse of the law by becoming a curse for us, for it is written: "Cursed is everyone who is hung on a tree"* --Galatians 3:13. We did everything under the sun. So it is by His stripes and His blood that washes us white as snow. *But now in Christ Jesus you who once were far away have been brought near through the blood of Christ* --Ephesians 2:13.

I will never forget that night because I was so high, and when I sobered up I was so ashamed of myself. I had about four hundred dollars and my friend had about nine, and she turned me out. That night took me to a whole other level of sexuality and drug use. It wasn't the last time I went to his house. I went back several times and I even took my son's father with me; we were all on drugs so it seemed natural to be dysfunctional.

It's sad how when you are in the dark, you really can't see the light at all. Thank You Jesus, for never taking Your eyes off me and coming to get me, and never letting me die in the mess and the filth. *So do not fear, for I am with you; do not be dismayed, for I am your God. I will strengthen you and help you; I will uphold you with my righteous right hand* --Isaiah 41:10. *For in the day of trouble he will keep me safe in his dwelling; he will hide me in the shelter of his tabernacle and set me high upon a rock* --Psalms 27:5.

So after I had my son I hooked up with my second's son's father. We were a heck of a match. He also had a cousin who liked to get high too. So we would sit up and get high all the time, playing dominoes, music, and just talking stuff. We thought it was fun back then. But like I said, thank God for Jesus.

We didn't have any kind of sexual contact, which was the best thing too. We actually partied like families do, when you get together and just laugh, tell jokes and love on one another. One thing I know about is once you open the doors to sex parties and over indulging, it's hard to close them again. You see, just when we were in the midst of all the crazy stuff we were doing, I got pregnant.

Eric was two years old, I was pregnant again and I felt trapped. Once again I didn't get high at all when I was pregnant. Yes I did smoke weed, I was still sick a lot and I couldn't keep food down, so it helped with the nausea. One thing about me was that I took care of my family at any cost, even if meant turning a trick or two. If I had to sell some drugs I would, if I had to lay with some people I really didn't want to, I would to put food on the table and keep the lights on.

All of the children's fathers were unemployed so I took care of them and the children too. Eric's dad stayed in and out of jail so much that it was his first home. He didn't have income to take care of himself or anyone else for that matter. Then Najee's father was a failure at hustling so he was his own best customer. We never saw any profit from any of our big drug deals. So I would end up prostituting myself out instead of him taking care of us. I took care of all of us.

We were both unemployed and going nowhere. My father invested in him starting a business as a landscaper but he drank beer all day and smoked weed so much that we didn't make any money at that either. So I decided to go to cosmetology school, and he decided to go to school too. I was in school by the time my son was six months old, and I loved it. I believe I lost respect for Najee's father and he lost respect for me too. But we were still getting high and not realizing we had nothing in common but sex, alcohol, and drugs and we shared a child too. But that was it. After a change of events and I realized that I could do bad all by myself, we broke up. I really thought that would be the end of my drug addiction but boy was I wrong. I stayed in my house for about eight more months. I had several roommates and I also had many lovers. I thank God everyday that he spared my life because I'm still here and I'm HIV free, Thank you Jesus!!!

So after I couldn't afford it any more I went back home to my fathers house. Little did I know that my son's father had moved in with him. He didn't tell me where he moved when we broke up. I found out by going over there to visit my dad and he was coming in from school. So I was living with him again and I thought we could hook up but it didn't work out like that. I believe at one time we loved each other but we had grown apart.

Now I'm next door to the neighbor girls again and I didn't want to be, so I tried hard not to get caught up with them again. It didn't work out like I planned. I started partying with the same people I said I wouldn't ever be with again. My partying got worse. I started staying out later and later. I was growing worse and fast. I was still going to school and I didn't take it seriously until it was time to graduate. I was so excited.

Remember now, I didn't graduate from high school, so this was a major accomplishment for me. Of course my father was excited too. So with everything that I was faced with, all of the enemy's schemes, I still graduated successfully. *Let us hold unswervingly to the hope we profess, for he who promised is faithful* --Hebrews 10:23. *So do not throw away your confidence; it will be richly rewarded* --Hebrews 10:35.

In May of 1994, I finished and committed everyday for the next few months to studying hard so I could pass the state boards examination. I realized I really wanted a career in cosmetology. The day I graduated was the first time I partied all night until the sun rose on a new day. That was supposed to have been my graduation party. When I think back I realize it was the worse night of my life. It started as a journey that would take me seventeen years to get off of. You never realize how addicted you are while you are there because there are other people in the same condition, who are right there with you.

Eventually my father turned my washroom into a salon and I owned my very first business. It was short-lived because my sister ended up stealing all my clients. I had to face it that she had way more experience than I did. She was talented and I didn't have enough experience. Not to mention, I overslept all the time from being up all night long. I was the cause of my problems, not my sister.

~ Chapter 7 ~

When I was about twenty-one years old, I was old enough to get into the nightclub. I went right to the club where my mother worked. This place was in Oakland, CA. I met some interesting men there. It was at this point I really started to do too much. I was in the after hours clubs in San Francisco and Oakland. I would be the taxi-cab for everyone who wanted a ride. As long as I could get high for free, they had a ride. I had money but not enough to party the way I wanted to party. I was so lost all I wanted to do was get high and party. I didn't think about the consequences or anything. Just being selfish.

If you're wondering where my children were, they were at home with my dad most of the time or with my girlfriends. I made sure they were always well taken care of. No matter how much I was tripping out in those streets, they were fine. My children always had the best clothes, they had food, and a clean roof over their heads. It's amazing how God can be taking care of you the whole time and you just don't see it because you don't know Him. Thank You Jesus for always keeping your eyes on me. *The Lord is gracious and compassionate, slow to anger and rich in love* -- Psalms 145:8. *For the LORD will be your*

confidence and will keep your foot from being snared --
Proverbs 3:26.

Now my mother lived with me and my father. We were
a happy little family, co-dependent and dysfunctional. I had
a wonderful job assisting as I came out of cosmetology
school. One was with a great friend. He became very
famous in Hollywood under another name, which we will
leave out for legal purposes. I still love him to this day, he's
a great friend. We partied a lot too. He had a lot of gay
friends, and we all got high. It's a trip, two out of every five
people got high in Richmond back then. Cocaine played a
major part in my life as a young woman growing up.
Almost all my friends got high, and sad to say, some still
do. I stayed up all night and I met a lot of men. Some were
good and some were just plain dogs. I started to go to
different clubs all the time mostly a lot of the after hour's
clubs. If you don't know what an after hours club is, it's a
place we go after the regular nightclub's would close. They
serve alcohol and anything else you might want. There was
every kind of illegal activity happening in there including
prostitution. You could stay in these places until the next
day and we wouldn't leave until the break of dawn. I
started to date a pimp who would spend his money on me
and his bottom girl would always ask who I was? He would

always tell her "you need to worry about getting my money not who I'm hanging out with."

I always thought that it was a trip how these women could go out and sell their bodies and then have the nerve to get jealous when their pimp was hanging out with another woman. It always seemed crazy to me to sell your body and then give the money to someone else. But no sin is greater than another. I was just as stupid because I was just getting drugs instead of the money.

I liked being in the after hours because it was a fast life. If everyone got high you didn't have to hide it. Everything was done out in the open and everyone was getting high until the sun came up.

Some years later when my father had a stroke, I thank You Lord I was there to call 911. We got him to the hospital in time. My father had a habit of taking laxatives, so they ate a hole in his small intestines. It was leaking bowel into his abdomen and that was scary. That is when I really started to get high even more. I believe it was stress too and I started to do it everyday because I was running from the pain of seeing him in pain.

I wasn't used to seeing my father like that, and it hurt a lot to watch him suffer. When my father came home, not long after, he had to have major surgery. I don't think I was ever sober again after that. I remember I had gotten my Section 8, subsidized housing and had to move. All I could get was a two-bedroom apartment in San Pablo, CA. By the time I moved in I was without a car and it was really hard being on my own for real. The car I had was a Jeep Cherokee that kept breaking down. So I had to function without a car because I couldn't afford to have it fixed anymore.

My father had his surgery and he was now living with my older sister Tina in Vallejo. He was one of kind and he knew I was getting high but he never said one word. I could do no wrong in his eyes. When he could, he would have my sister bring him to my house to see me and the boys. We really missed each other.

I'm so glad my father never saw me doing what I was doing, because he would have probably left this earth sooner from a heart attack. To God be the glory for letting him stay a few more years. When my father got well enough he moved back in with me and the kids, I still had a few clients that would come and get their hair done at the house. So I still had a little money coming in but not like before. I had stopped getting high so much partly because I couldn't afford it and I had no car to get around with anyway. I had a few friends but not enough to help me support my drug habit like the friends I had before.

After my father actually moved in was when I started to have money again. He wanted to be able to get back and forth to his friends house to book horses again, and he was really bored at my sister's house.

Before I knew it, I was on my way back to getting high on a regular basis. Here's how it all happened. I was taking care of the kids during the week and my father suggested that I call some of my friends and go out. So here we go, I started with the bad habits again. I had my delivery contact and I lived around the corner from the liquor store. It was on again. My dad would keep the kids. They were good and that's why my father didn't mind taking care of them, not to mention they were his only grandkids. So when he would shop for himself he would shop for them too. He loved his boys. We had them on a schedule. They would go to school in the morning and then to bed early at night. They were no trouble at all. I had it made, unemployed and on dope. Boy what a life.

~ *Chapter 8* ~

One day my girlfriend suggested that I work for an escort service. She said, you give it up for free when you go out on your dates so you might as well get you some money for it. So I tried it out. Thank God for His grace and mercy. *Free me from the trap that is set for me, for you are my refuge* --Psalms 31:4. *The salvation of the righteous comes from the LORD; he is their stronghold in time of trouble* -- Psalms 37:39. I only worked for three weeks. I would get picked up by her, or some of the men would pick me up. I didn't like it at all. You know when you don't fit in so I knew when to quit, and that was quickly.

By now you are probably saying, this girl has had a rough life, and you're right. But God. *But thanks be to God! He gives us the victory through our Lord Jesus Christ* --1Corinthians 15:57. By the time I was twenty-five I had slept with so many men and women that it's nothing but God's grace that I don't have HIV. In spite of everything I was going through, I still wanted to sing. It was dying to come out of me.

Soon after, my lonely days were over when I met a man who moved in with me and my dad very quickly. He was nice but not for me. I realized I was lonely because I never had a childhood. I was raising kids and really never grew up myself. I felt like I had no identity. Then the more I got high, I developed a bad habit of picking my face which was called tweaking. That's a whole other story that goes back at least a couple years prior to me having my own house. We will get to that story later in the book. Let's keep it moving forward.

The man who moved in was nice, he just didn't understand that I was going through withdrawals. I hadn't gotten high for about three months but when I did he would say, you aren't going to bed yet? You need to get some sleep. Boy if he only knew I wish I could have, but I was just too high to relax.

He kept asking me when I was going to get a job. So I did. I got a job working in a salon with my sister. I didn't have very many clients so I worked as an assistant too. I think he expected me to be making a whole lot of money right off the top. Not so. He had purchased a BMW from a used car dealer. The car was a lemon so we ended up spending more money than the car was worth. When he would ask me how much money I was making it was because after he moved in, he was paying bills, shelling out money for groceries and taking care of two kids. He basically bit off more than he could chew. Not to mention I wanted to go back to my old lifestyle of using drugs. Needless to say he moved out shortly after we had a huge argument. It was loud and very ugly. The kids were screaming, and it wasn't pretty.

Then two days later, believe it or not, this Negro and some old lady he was seeing, moved in with his brother downstairs. I couldn't believe he pulled a move like that; it appeared to me that he already had that relationship going on before he left me. Of course I couldn't let that ride, so I quietly went downstairs and put his tires on flats. That's what any foolish, scorned woman would do, right? I had been drinking and that devil got the best of me that night. But I would never pull a move like that ever again. The God I serve now will fight all my battles. Amen. *He will cover you with his feathers, and under his wings you will find refuge; his faithfulness will be your shield and rampart* --Psalms 91:4. *I know that you are pleased with me, for my enemy does not triumph over me. In my integrity you uphold me and set me in your presence forever* --Psalms 41:11-12. *And having disarmed the powers and authorities, he made a public spectacle of them, triumphing over them by the cross* --Colossians 2:15.

I was so high and drunk that I popped one tire and since no noise came out, I decided to pop another, then one more.

The last tire made this loud popping sound. Wrong move. I ran up the stairs but they made noise as I was aiming to get back into my apartment. He automatically knew it was me and had the nerve to call the police on me, like he wasn't wrong for shacking up with that new woman right after we broke up! He had his nerve! Isn't it funny how when you know you're wrong, you always want to blame the other person for your mistakes. We always say he made me do it. No the enemy puts the thought in your head and you decide to run with it.

We have a choice to stand still and see the salvation of the Lord or act on the enemy's devices that are meant to destroy everything God is doing in our lives. *Then, led by Jehoshaphat, all the men of Judah and Jerusalem returned joyfully to Jerusalem, for the LORD had given them cause to rejoice over their enemies* --2Chronicles 20:27. *Praise be to the Lord my Rock, who trains my hands for war, my fingers for battle* --Psalms 144:1. So when the police came, of course I lied, but he wouldn't let up so I confessed. I promised to replace the tires on the first of the month, you know, when I get my check. Jesus, the Father, and the Holy Ghost have always taken care of me. *Do not be like them, for your Father knows what you need before you ask him* -- Matthews 6:8. What a mighty God we serve. His mercies are new every morning. *Do not withhold your mercy from me, O LORD; may your love and your truth always protect me* --Psalms 40:11. He was taking care of me, loving me even when I was acting a fool. *Who redeems your life from the pit and crowns you with love and compassion* --Psalms 103:4. I love you so much Lord.

~ *Chapter 9* ~

Fast forward to six months later. I started hanging out with a girl who stayed downstairs. So one night we decided to go to Oakland to a club where my mother worked. We had a good time and we stayed there until the club closed and of course I wanted to go to the after hours. My mom said she wasn't going to the after hours, but we could get a ride from her friend. So that's what we did. Naturally I bought some stuff and it was on. My friend stayed at the bar area as I moved all around the club. I loved the atmosphere of the after hours clubs. I somehow convinced myself that I was important. A ghetto superstar! I believed it was all about me, and the world revolved around me--at least that's what I believed. Well our ride left us stranded and we had to figure out how we would make it home. There was a guy who kept getting on my nerves at the bar, not to mention he was silly too, so I ended up cussing him out really bad. You will not believe who gave us a ride home. He did.

My girlfriend had been talking to his friend and she got us the ride home. When I first got to the car, I looked and said, Wow it's this guy. In addition, there were about five other men who were all merchant seaman docked at Jack

London Square in Oakland. We wound up getting a ride but in the opposite direction, to San Pablo, the border of Richmond. You would think I would have been thankful? No! I was still talking crazy to the guy the whole time on the way home.

See, the Lord still takes care of you when you don't have sense enough to take care of yourself. To God be the glory. He takes care of you even when you don't deserve it. *The Lord is good to all; he has compassion on all he has made* --Psalms 145:9.

Well the man who gave us the ride home would end up being the man I would spend the next nine years of my life with. His name was Alton, and he was a very sweet man when I look back, but at that time in my life I was all about money, drugs, and using people. If I could take back the things I did in the past, I would. Even though I treated him like he was nothing, there was still something about me that he loved. I would have to say that it was the Lord-- it was nothing special about me, but everything special about Jesus.

Alton took so much stuff off me that he could have been called a martyr. He spent all his money all the time. He bought whatever I wanted and how much I wanted. You see the enemy wanted me to overdose a few times, but the

Lord had a plan all the time. Alton took me shopping, dancing, and there was no limit to what he would do for me. You see I wasn't in my right mind, so what I thought I needed I actually didn't. But God, His grace and mercy was holding me all the time.

I admit that was how my addiction took a turn for the worse. Alton and I would stay up all night and all day. My dad was staying with us too and I believe he knew what was going on all the time but he just turned a deaf ear to it. Lord help me to always change the things I can and courage to know when to change and wisdom to know the difference. *Whether you turn to the right or to the left, your ears will hear a voice behind you, saying, "This is the way; walk in it."* --Isaiah 30:21. *Surely you desire truth in the inner parts; you teach me wisdom in the inmost place --* Psalms 51:6.

We were so dysfunctional. Alton and I would fight and then make up right away. That's how you know when you have reached a point of no return, just doing stupid things. I thought me and that man were all right until I started listening to the young people in the building and started disrespecting myself by disrespecting him in front of people all the time.

Then I thought I was slick too and started dating this young man who lived in the apartment building. In my mind I was so smart, but really I was very young and foolish. That boy couldn't even buy a bag of potato chips. I believe most of the things we go through are through generational curses so we have to fight really hard to overcome. Thinking I was a so-called player, I stopped letting him come over whenever he wanted to like in the beginning. He had to call first. Sometimes after going out with Alton, I would spend time with this young boy when I got home. How lost I was and actually gone off cocaine, but just didn't know it then.

I think when I saw Alton smoke crack, like what I was doing was any better, I lost a lot of respect for him. But you know dope is dope. It doesn't matter what kind of drug you use, drugs are drugs. None is better than the other. One day his friends sold him some when we were hanging out and I will never forget that night. We had just left the club and he wanted to go over to the friend's house. I was wearing all black: shirt, shoes, and pants. We were so high that at first it seemed like I was tweaking, but I wasn't, these people had lice. That was my first and only experience with lice. Yes, you heard me right those people had lice. Talk about nasty. I was furious, because I had on brand new clothes, this Negro was smoking crack, and I thought I was too fine to even be there with them. God has a way of showing you that you are no better than any one else. You are in the same pit as they are. Same dope fiend. I tweaked out and picked my face from that time on. Thank You Lord for delivering me from the sin I was sinking deep into. *Send forth your light and your truth, let them guide me; let them bring me to your holy mountain, to the place where you dwell* --Psalms 43:3. If I had ten thousand tongues it still wouldn't be enough to give you all praise and glory that is due your name. *May my lips overflow with praise, for you teach me your decrees* --Psalms 119:171.

I never went with Alton to that house again and I told him he couldn't go over there and stay anymore either. After that episode I couldn't get high without wiping my face with alcohol. Needless to say we were tweaking buddies for a long time. I still don't know why he stayed with me as long as he did. He was called every name but the name God gave him, yet he stayed with me.

~ *Chapter 10* ~

After about a year I got tired of being used by the apartment complex and the young man. It's funny how all the time I thought I was using him, he was using me. He was sleeping with the young girl downstairs and taking my money and spending it on her. Talking about reaping what you sow, we had a little soap opera going on. I remember crying out to God about my life. I wanted to change but I just didn't know how. Thank You Lord for patience and for always covering me even when I didn't know you were covering me.

One day momma called and said that there was an apartment available across the street from her. She lived in Emeryville at the time. It was a two bedroom, with one and a half bathrooms. I thought I was really stepping up my game at the time and I was really excited about it too. What I thought was the biggest mistake of my life was really the beginning of my journey back to God. *Though he stumble, he will not fall, for the LORD upholds him with his hand* -- Psalms 37:24.

We moved a month later. It was me, my two boys and my father. We had just enough room. Later my father decided to move in with my momma across the street. My sister Fleta had moved to Los Angeles, my mom was in her place with my dad and a friend who stayed from time to time. But before I moved I visited my sister Tina's church and wound up accepting Jesus as my Lord and Savior. It was Easter Sunday, which turned out to be the last Easter I would spend with my father. I remember my dad had bought the boys these beautiful grey suits, complete with Easter baskets. We took pictures that morning before we went to church. I even joined my sister's church that Sunday as well.

I still find God to be so amazing that He still knocks at our hearts door, even when we don't understand it. He still loves in spite of us. He is so wonderful, awesome, amazing, magnificent, and worthy to be praised. *And he passed in front of Moses, proclaiming, "The LORD, the LORD, the compassionate and gracious God, slow to anger, abounding in love and faithfulness," --*Exodus 34:6. God had a call for my life a long time ago; He called me out of darkness into His marvelous light. *For he has rescued us from the dominion of darkness and brought us into the kingdom of the Son he loves, --*Colossians 1:13. No one explained that it wouldn't get easier, in fact it would get even harder. That's what happens with someone who receives Christ as Lord of their life. We have to know that we don't do it alone anymore; the battle is not ours, it's the Lords. *He said: "Listen, King Jehoshaphat and all who live in Judah and Jerusalem! This is what the LORD says to you: 'Do not be afraid or discouraged because of this vast army. For the battle is not yours, but God's* --2Chronicles 20:15.

I believe that if I had a better understanding of what I needed to do, then I would have changed a long time ago. Thank God He had a plan already in place just in case I didn't have proper ministry to help me on my new journey. He is such a Gentleman, He only wants a relationship with us, you, me, this human race. He created us in His image so that's why we were created to worship Him, to praise Him, to give Him glory. *God is spirit, and his worshipers must worship in spirit and in truth.* --John 4:24.

I mean no harm to the pastor that God used to get me into the kingdom a long time ago, but there was no plan in place for me to really change my life. I was even baptized a month later. But because it wasn't explained to me that the battle didn't belong to me, it belonged to the Lord, I ended up trying to fight my battles alone. I had no clue about the weapons of our warfare. So when I fought, I lost some battles and the war was far from over.

I still really miss my earthly father, as I write down these memories. I still remember crying so much to the point that I could hardly see my way. I look back and see how much time was spent on getting high and wasting precious time. Thank God there was a purpose for the pain. I think back on how much more time could have been spent with the kids and my dad. One thing about my dad, he was one of a kind. Now I spend as much time as I can with the children. I thank God that I will see dad again one day in glory. *The city does not need the sun or the moon to shine on it, for the glory of God gives it light, and the Lamb is its lamp. The nations will walk by its light, and the kings of the earth will bring their splendor into it* --Revelations 21:23-24.

~ *Chapter 11* ~

I remember there was a man that held me hostage in Sausalito, CA. I don't remember how we met but I thought he was a gentleman, but oh was I wrong. He smoked crack for one and when he started getting high that night, it was like night and day. Then there was a fireman in Oakland, who knew what kind of fires he was putting out and ones he could set. I remember he took me out to eat and after dinner he asked if I got high and when I said yes, he pulled out this big bag of dope. Man I always seemed to attract those type of men back then. When I look back on my life, Jesus kept me in the midst of it all. *In his heart a man plans his course, but the LORD determines his steps* --Proverbs 16:9. When I moved to Emeryville, I always stayed in the house. I had so much company at times I had to act like I wasn't at home sometimes. I kept a package of drugs and was known for having something all the time. Thanksgiving came and went, then Christmas and New Years came and went.

There was coke party after coke party. On February 1, 1999, is when my dad passed away. When he did, I was at my son's father's house. We were up all night and it was about three or four in the morning. I remember my father had asked me to bring the boys to the hospital to see him. He was in there with pneumonia and I told him I would bring them the next day. Well the next day never came for him or us. You see, I believe he knew it was time to go home to be with the Father. I was just too selfish and lazy when I didn't take the boys to the hospital to see him. I believe if I would have done it they would be different children. Maybe?

God always knew who we would all be. He knew before the foundations of the earth were formed who we all were going to be and what we would do. He thought about us all. *Your eyes saw my unformed body. All the days ordained for me were written in your book before one of them came to be* --Psalms 139:16. *The people I formed for myself that they may proclaim my praise* --Isaiah 43:21.

I will never forget that day for the rest of my life. I still carry the pain deep in my heart. The guilt has faded, but the pain remains. Dad asked me to bring the boys and some salt. I brought the salt instead of the children. I was tweaking and watching porno when my mom and Aunt Barbara came to get me. Talk about denial. I had this addiction that seemed to only medicate the problem. I never really grieved at all. I just self-medicated and stayed numb to life all the time.

For the next year I continued to worsen. I had my father's ashes and from time to time I would take them out and cry over them. So I thank the Lord for allowing me to go through the healing and grieving process that the enemy had stolen from me over twelve years ago. I truly miss my best friend, my father and to be honest I had writers block for a long time because of the pain. A few months after his death, I got pregnant. This pregnancy was different because I was a dope fiend mother.

~ *Chapter 12* ~

I was pregnant and trying, I mean really trying to stop getting high. There was always something happening that I felt I just couldn't pass up. You see I really wasn't ready to have my third son, but he was here so I had to make some adjustments to prepare for him. The Holy Spirit said I was ready to have him. My child's father was an older man so he seemed to get on my nerves all the time, and he never stopped me from getting high. Now I realize I was a grown woman and I made the choices so it wasn't his fault. But I regarded it as a weakness for him to just sit around and allow someone to get high who is pregnant with your child. In fact, he supported my habit at the beginning of my pregnancy. He wasn't able to give me the support I needed to stop doing drugs during this stage of my life. I really wanted to but didn't have the necessary support to stop. I didn't step outside of my comfort zone to try to get the help either. To make matters worse, he gave me a venereal disease while I was pregnant too. So I really lost a lot of respect for him after that.

I'm so glad that God is not a man. *God is not a man, that he should lie, nor a son of man, that he should change his mind. Does he speak and then not act? Does he promise and not fulfill?* --Numbers 23:19. The word of God says judge not lest ye also be judged in that same manner you judge. *Do not judge, and you will not be judged. Do not condemn, and you will not be condemned. Forgive, and you will be forgiven* --Luke 6:37. What right did I have to be acting like I was better than him but I did. Thank God for Jesus. *When pride comes, then comes disgrace, but with humility comes wisdom* --Proverbs 11:2.

My brother from my adopted sister had just come home from jail, and as always, I gave him a place to stay. One day he was supposed to give me a ride to pickup my food stamps. Yeah, I was on welfare back then. Anyway he sent his friend instead because he wasn't going to get off work in enough time for me to get them before the check cashing place closed. This friend was so fine to me and it was love at first sight for both of us. I think. He gave me a ride, bought me some chicken and gave me his phone number. The rest is history. So after that I called him for a ride all the time. He would visit and I would cook for him because he loved my cooking. By now I was about six months pregnant and he would hang out with me and my brother all the time. I fell in love quickly. I think back and realize I was pregnant and full of emotions, and yes I was on the rebound and lonely. I had broken up with my son's father a few months earlier. I was really trying not to get high, but it was hard for me to stop. I got a job working as a cocktail waitress at this nightclub, wrong, wrong! See the devil is really slick, he would pull out drugs in front of you that will trip you up if you don't know Jesus. I wasn't walking with the Lord back then anyway. So when I fell, I fell hard in my addiction. My godsister would say, come and get high, it's all right. I had done it all the time with my kids and they turned out fine. See how the enemy will trick you? But remember God allowed it, He knew He would bring me out and my children out of it. *Jesus looked at them and said, "With man this is impossible, but with God all things are possible."* --Matthews 19:26.

She wasn't the only one getting high with me either. There were other people in my complex getting high with me too. I was in the pit for real. I thank God for His grace and His mercy because I delivered a healthy baby boy. *The LORD is a refuge for the oppressed, a stronghold in times of trouble* --Psalms 9:9. I was so grateful that the hospital didn't keep my son, God's precious gift, and take him away from me. He is so good to me; I'm talking about God the Father.

I realized something while I was with this other man. It's that men who let their woman stay on drugs usually have something to hide themselves. After I had my third son I was clean for a minute. I went back to work immediately three months later. My new man had lost his job and I had to hold it down once again. Then my third son's father who had been sending me money from his job on the ship got kicked off for a dirty drug test. Now you're probably saying, this girl really made bad choices in men and in life. I wasn't saved then, so of course I made some bad decisions. I made decisions on my own, not asking for help from the Holy Ghost, or my heavenly Father, or Jesus my Big Brother.

My life was spinning out of control. My new man was cheating on me while I was working at the post office at night during the Christmas season. He would drop me off because I worked the night shift until five in the morning, and he would do God knows what while I was gone. He sneaked people in my house while the kids were upstairs sleeping. He made them go to bed early so he could do whatever he was doing in the house.

Shortly after the post office job was up, I got another job working at Supercuts with normal working hours. I loved going out so I would get my tips and go out after work sometimes. This Negro was so crazy that he would sneak people in the house and when I was on my way home

I wouldn't call to let him know I was on my way. He would act real suspicious and try to fake being asleep. My heart and my spirit always told me different though. It is amazing how the enemy will play with your life when you're not walking with God. I always felt like I was surrounded by demons so when I came to know Christ for myself, I realized that's what I was dealing with.

As I would come in the house through the front door, he would take forever taking the chain off the door, and I knew people would be going out the back door. Amazing things can be going on right under your nose but you just can't prove it at that moment. The enemy always thinks he's one step ahead of you.

He would always say I was crazy or just tripping of course. I was never able to prove what I thought was happening. There was one time me and his friend went to the strip club. Well I will leave out that information. But all we did was go to the club and his girlfriend found out and wanted to fight me. I think she thought that I had done something with the both of them, which was a lie birthed out of hell. We fought and we had a good run in, but I broke my hand in the process. It's still so amazing the way God looks out for you even when you don't know He's looking out for you. *For I will forgive their wickedness and will remember their sins no more.*" --Hebrews 8:12.

It's true once you're His, He never turns His back on you

because He took care of me back then. *As far as the east is*

from the west, so far has he removed our transgressions

from us --Psalms 103:12.

I had just made it past probation at Supercuts, and they

paid me disability anyway. They didn't have to but they

did. What an awesome God we serve! We can't go too far

for Him to come and get us. He's everywhere. Even in

darkness He's there. *But thanks be to God, who always*

leads us in triumphal procession in Christ and through us

spreads everywhere the fragrance of the knowledge of him

--2Corinthians 2:14. He always has a way for your escape.

No temptation has seized you except what is common to

man. And God is faithful; he will not let you be tempted

beyond what you can bear. But when you are tempted, he

will also provide a way out so that you can stand up under

it --1Corinthians 10:13.

In the midst of already being in a troubled relationship,

this Negro gets bold. He and his friend started calling my

cousin over while I was at work. Now my cousin happens

to be none other than the professional prostitute who got

caught with that famous actor in Hollywood years ago – I

will leave her name out for legal reasons but you all know

who they were. Anyway, they were just down right disrespectful to me, all three of them. I still don't know the full details of everything they were doing. I believe God gives you just enough to realize that's not where He wants you to be. *He who walks with the wise grows wise, but a companion of fools suffers harm* --Proverbs 13:20. There were all sorts of red flags that I ignored but I'm glad I did finally listen. Then a year later I had a beautiful baby girl.

It was time to move again because there wasn't enough space for everybody. This time we moved to Hayward to a beautiful three-bedroom house. Yes, a house this time. I thank God for allowing everything to happen according to His plan. *In you I trust, O my God. Do not let me be put to shame, nor let my enemies triumph over me* --Psalms 25:2. But I still had a habit that I could not stop now for real. You can run from the people but you can't run from you. I tried to stay away from drugs but I just couldn't control myself. I knew I wasn't supposed to be getting high while I was pregnant but I couldn't do it on my own. I was too proud to receive help from the doctor because I started to test dirty at the doctor's office at my prenatal visits. So they made me see a social worker. Just by the grace of God they didn't take my child from me. *I know that you are pleased with me, for my enemy does not triumph over me* --Psalms

41:11. Even in the midst of all my supposed to be friends and family that allowed me to get high anyway, I thank God. He kept my daughter's mind and my life in the palm of His hands. My life was falling apart and fast too. God had me right where He needed me to be. *You gave me life and showed me kindness, and in your providence watched over my spirit* --Job 10:12. After I had my child, there was a man I use to hang out with. Just thinking about him makes my stomach uneasy. He would give me an unlimited supply of dope as long as I was, well you use your imagination. To this day I still believe this man was a demon. As for my daughter's father, he got worse with his addiction to sex and internet porn.

He was still sneaking people in and out of windows and back doors at the new house too. Although I never caught him, I still get sick to my stomach thinking about how he continued to let me get high even when I was pregnant and after I had the baby. He used me to take care of him financially, physically, and emotionally. I was being used and everywhere I turned, someone was using me. You probably say what gave me the right to be upset. I was out getting high all the time anyway. You see the difference between me and others was that I really did want to be normal and I tried to be, but those other people wanted to be wrong and they did other people wrong besides me.

I was addicted to drugs but I wanted to know what their excuses were? I had snakes all around me. I had shown my girlfriends where the dope man's house was. But when I went into the hospital to deliver my daughter, her father's excuse for his absence was he had to pickup a camera from his dad's house in El Sobrante (past Richmond). Instead, he was giving rides to my "supposed" friends to the dope man's house. I had whores for friends and the fathers of my children were whores too! I have had some emotionally draining relationships in my life. But for the grace of God, there go I. *For surely, O LORD, you bless the righteous; you surround them with your favor as with a shield --* Psalms 5:12.

So after that happened with the ride and unexplained missing time, I never brought it up to him again but knew it would never be the same again. We lived in a world of sin but you reap what you sow as I have been saying throughout this book. Everything we did apart from each other, the more it came back to haunt us when we were together. I wouldn't pay to go back into that life. Those demons are nothing to play with. So if you know anyone struggling with drugs, alcohol, or any type of addictions, pray, fast, stay in the Lords presence on their behalf. *And pray in the Spirit on all occasions with all kinds of prayers and requests. With this in mind, be alert and always keep on praying for all the saints* --Ephesians 6:18. They are not in there because they want to be, some people really do want to be free. They just can't do it on their own. They need all the help they can get. There is not a day that goes by that I don't thank the Lord for saving me and my family from myself and from the enemy. *Therefore, if anyone is in Christ, he is a new creation; the old has gone, the new has come! --2*Corinthians 5:17. You see the enemy was in me, and God saved me from my wicked, wicked ways. God had been calling me out of darkness into His marvelous light the whole time. *Men will dwell again in his shade. He will flourish like the grain. He will blossom like a vine, and his fame will be like the wine from Lebanon* --Hosea 14:7. I would always ask my daughter's father when we were going to get married. He told me on my birthday. Well you know, my birthday came and went, so thank God He kept me when I couldn't keep myself. He always wants the best for His children. *Then your light will break forth like the dawn, and your healing will quickly appear; then your righteousness will go before you, and the glory of the LORD will be your rear guard* --Isaiah 58:8.

~ *Chapter 13* ~

Another six months later, my addiction got really out of
control. I was chasing after the high all the time. When I
look back now I realize I was unhappy with myself, my life
and my relationships. I would be on all nighters all the
time, but I never stopped working and never stopped
paying all the bills. I was the provider for the family. My
man didn't work so somebody had to do it. I was not going
to go without, and neither were the children. He wasn't the
problem, it was really me. I left the house for hours at a
time, sometimes for a whole day. He was at home but was
unhappy too. I believe we were both insecure with each
other and we were both lonely, trying to make a bad
situation better, all without the help of the Lord. *The
blessing of the LORD brings wealth, and he adds no
trouble to it* --Proverbs 10:22. *But seek first his kingdom
and his righteousness, and all these things will be given to
you as well* --Matthews 6:33. So as he would sneak people
in while I was gone, I would get high all night.

I never really felt like I was loved at home. I was lied to
consistently, promises were never kept, I was cheating and
being cheating on. I remember finding earring backs on the
carpet and lipstick on the front door knob. Yeah things

were crazy but through it all God remained faithful to His word and kept me when I couldn't keep myself. *And the God of all grace, who called you to his eternal glory in Christ, after you have suffered a little while, will himself restore you and make you strong, firm and steadfast* -- 1Peter 5:10. My daughter's father told me I was tweaking because he knew I was high. One thing I know is when people have their own set of issues including me, we tend to take the focus off of ourselves to hide our issues. When I wanted to stay home he would start fights so I would leave the house. He made me unhappy on purpose because he knew what buttons to push. So even though I knew what he was doing I wouldn't actually get it until I was already out of the house and in panic mode.

We also had a janitorial business back then. He was making only one hundred and sixty dollars a month from one contract we had. When he was supposed to be cleaning buildings and wouldn't come back for six to seven hours it would tick me off. The reason why is because he wasn't cleaning, he was messing off. I paid all the bills so I figured what right did he have to want to have any type of fun. How selfish addiction can be. You think because you make all the money, you have the right to control people and their lives. Well anyway I just wanted to go out and get high. It's not that he didn't know, because he was following me. Remember I said he was stalking me earlier.

When he came home one night I was mad and we started arguing and before you knew it, we were fighting. When he hit me, I hit him back but then I wound up with a cut on my face just above my eye. He took off in the car. My mom stayed with us at the time, so when she came home I was bleeding and she took me to the hospital where I had to have stitches. My life was never the same after that night. When we arrived at the hospital, they asked how I got the cut. I lied as most victims of abuse do. I said I bumped my head on the table. Let's be clear, we were both victims. I was on drugs, and he was unhappy too. There is always two sides to every story, and you would have to read his book if he decides to write about his side of this story. Anyway, what the devil meant for bad the Lord will turn it around to bless you. God had to remove both of us from each others lives so He could get both of our attention. *Then they cried out to the Lord in their trouble, and he delivered them from their distress* --Psalms 107:6. I was unaware that my mother had called the police. When they showed up I had already left the house in her car for the rest of the evening. I wound up getting high and playing the victim at the dope man's house. I told my mother I was going out to get some cigarettes, but didn't come back until five in the morning, high of course. I wasn't there ten minutes before the police were at my door again. At the time I thought my mother was trying to set me up to lose my children. To God be the glory. Not even the weapons we form against ourselves shall prosper. *No weapon forged against you will prevail, and you will refute every tongue that accuses you. This is the heritage of the servants of the LORD, and this is their vindication from me," declares the Lord* --Isaiah 54:17. The doctor said it looked like a fist had hit me, not me bumping my head on the table.

Then my addiction grew worse. My man knew I was bleeding when he left that night, and I believe he was afraid and He never came back that night either. As I gave my report to the police that morning I was still high. I believe God was showing me His strength, because there is no way I was supposed to have kept my kids in the midst of everything I was going through. *He ransoms me unharmed from the battle waged against me, even though many oppose me* --Psalms 55:18. God was getting ready to show me that I didn't need that man, all I needed was Him, the Lord almighty. *And the ransomed of the LORD will return. They will enter Zion with singing; everlasting joy will crown their heads. Gladness and joy will overtake them, and sorrow and sighing will flee away* --Isaiah 35:10. God had been taking care of me the whole time anyway. He allowed the police to see someone who was hurt and damaged and not someone high and tweaking that morning when I look back.

My daughter's father knew he was headed for jail. So when he came home we talked and he turned himself in, because he was still on probation at the time. When he went to jail I went on longer binges. As I type these words all I can see is the time that passed and the precious time that was wasted back then. It really breaks my heart to know all the memories from my children's lives that I missed.

To this very day I don't believe that my daughter's father ever loved me. I believe he needed me but not that he loved me. I visited him in jail but he was such a liar that I don't even know if I was the only one visiting him. You see, it doesn't take long to know if you want to marry someone, even if they have issues. You do your best to try to help them, no matter what the situation is. You want to see them at their best, that's what I did with him. That's how we started the janitorial business, so he could create his own job. No one would hire him, so we made a job for him. I truly loved him, in spite of the issues I had, I really wanted him to shine. That's what you do when you love someone, you try to help them do better and whatever it takes, you will do it.

~ *Chapter 14* ~

Fast forward to about four months down the line. I had been on so many all nighters that my older children had become my new babysitters. My mother left me in my addiction all alone at the house. She wouldn't offer me any type of help or show any type of concern for me. That is exactly how the enemy works, he will cause confusion and then he will call child protective services on you, instead of helping you out of the pit. God said no, this is my child and I will have my way. You will live and not die. Instead He said I love you. He will help point out all your weaknesses. He will lend a helping hand, without wanting anything in return. *Once you were alienated from God and were enemies in your minds because of your evil behavior. But now he has reconciled you by Christ's physical body through death to present you holy in his sight, without blemish and free from accusation-- if you continue in your faith, established and firm, not moved from the hope held out in the gospel. This is the gospel that you heard and that has been proclaimed to every creature under heaven, and of which I, Paul, have become a servant* --Colossians 1:21-23. *Though he stumble, he will not fall, for the LORD upholds him with his hand* --Psalms 37:24. That's how God works; He's always standing right there waiting for you to ask for help. He says, I stand at the door. If you open up I will enter in. *Here I am! I stand at the door and knock. If anyone hears my voice and opens the door, I will come in and eat with him, and he with me* --Revelations 3:20. He's always waiting to help His children if we just ask Him for the help we need.

So when I look back at my life I thank my older children for looking after the babies even when I couldn't. They stood right there with me, in the gap for me. Thank You Lord for these awesome gifts from You. And if you train up a child in the way they should go, they won't depart. *Train a child in the way he should go, and when he is old he will not turn from it* --Proverbs 22:6. God gifted my children with His strength, His wisdom, and His spirit; I don't believe they would have been able to do it on their own, not without Him leading and guiding them. *Sons are a heritage from the Lord, children a reward from him. Like arrows in the hands of a warrior are sons born in one's youth. Blessed is the man whose quiver is full of them. They will not be put to shame when they contend with their enemies in the gate* --Psalms 127:3-5. They persevered in spite of everything that was going on around them. I remember going to church on Mother's Day in 2002. To this day I still thank the Lord for my girlfriend Kendra Williams. He used her to get me to where He needed me to be. That day I gave my life to Christ for the last and final time. I mention her by name because she was available to be used by God. Thank You Lord for her life and continue to bless your daughter in Jesus name Amen.

We went to First A.M.E. in Oakland, California. God met right there, and that was the beginning of the most beautiful relationship you could ever share with anyone, or should I say the blessed Trinity. *In that day their burden will be lifted from your shoulders, their yoke from your neck; the yoke will be broken because you have grown so fat* --Isaiah 10:27. The only thing I would like for the minister to say when you give your life to Christ is to mention that it doesn't get easier, it get's harder. It's just not your battle anymore, it's the Lords. *Then no harm will befall you, no disaster will come near your tent. For he will command his angels concerning you to guard you in all your ways; they will lift you up in their hands, so that you will not strike your foot against a stone* --Psalms 91:10-12. So I joined church and got saved all at the same time. So by my not knowing that the battle had just begun, I really believed it would get better but not before it got worse. I remember partying harder than I had ever done before I got saved. The more I wanted to do right, I did wrong. It's like Paul said, the very thing that I don't want to do, I do. The very thing I ought to do, I don't. *We know that the law is spiritual; but I am unspiritual, sold as a slave to sin. I do not understand what I do. For what I want to do I do not do, but what I hate I do. And if I do what I do not want to do, I agree that the law is good. As it is, it is no longer I myself who do it, but it is sin living in me. I know that nothing good lives in me, that is, in my sinful nature. For I have the desire to do what is good, but I cannot carry it out. For what I do is not the good I want to do; no, the evil I do not want to do--this I keep on doing. Now if I do what I do not want to do, it is no longer I who do it, but it is sin living in me that does it. So I find this law at work: When I want to do good, evil is right there with me. For in my inner being I delight in God's law; but I see another law at work in the members of my body, waging war against the law of my mind and making me a prisoner of the law of sin at work within my members. What a wretched man I am! Who will rescue me from this body of death? Thanks be to God--through Jesus Christ our Lord! So then, I myself in my mind am a slave to God's law, but in the sinful nature a slave to the law of sin* --Romans 7:14-25. My heart breaks to even recall those memories, but I know someone will be set free if they just hear that they are not the only ones struggling with the same issues I had before I gave my life to Christ.

Even after doing so, it was still a battle. Now I know that I know it's not my battle, it belongs to the Lord. *But this is what the LORD says: "Yes, captives will be taken from warriors, and plunder retrieved from the fierce; I will contend with those who contend with you, and your children I will save* --Isaiah 49:25.

I thank the Lord for his grace and mercy, that my children were never taken and I didn't die in my addiction either. Know that just because you're a good mother or a good father, it doesn't make you immune to the enemy's scheme, or devices. He really does come to kill, steal, and destroy. *The thief comes only to steal and kill and destroy; I have come that they may have life, and have it to the full* -- John 10:10. He doesn't want anyone to make it to heaven. Jesus said that He desires that none should perish. *The Lord is not slow in keeping his promise, as some understand slowness. He is patient with you, not wanting anyone to perish, but everyone to come to repentance* –2 Peter 3:9. That's what I love about God, He will allow you to fall but there is nowhere you can go that He won't come and get you. Yes, He loves us that much. He knew He was going to get glory out of my life and losing my kids at that point would have actually destroyed me instead of making me stronger.

He also knew I was strong enough to pull through, with His help of course. *The salvation of the righteous comes from the LORD; he is their stronghold in time of trouble* -- Psalms 37:39. There were so many things that happened and there was another moment in particular that I remember well. I had been up on a binge for about two days at a man's house in Pinole, CA. He sold drugs too. He was the kind of man that would feed you drugs all day long, as long as, well you can use your imagination. I call them predators. Some are just very insecure, they know they would never get a good looking woman any other way so they use drugs to get you. They believe that no one would love them for who they really are.

Anyway I remember going home and the kids had been with my son's father, and they were having breakfast. I was still getting high and I went downstairs drinking some wine and the next thing I knew I was having a minor stroke. I was doing something I had no business doing in the family room. My hands went numb first, then my feet started to tingle too. I was overdosing on cocaine, and I remember calling on Jesus. *And everyone who calls on the name of the*

LORD will be saved; for on Mount Zion and in Jerusalem there will be deliverance, as the LORD has said, among the survivors whom the LORD calls --Joel 2:32. I said to Him, Lord if you get me out of this I will never go back to this place again. I called to my son's father to call an ambulance. He was saying all kinds of crazy things to the operator but I told him to tell the truth so they could help me.

Again there was God taking care of me. *They cried to you and were saved; in you they trusted and were not disappointed* --Psalms 22:5. Before they got there, my son's father put me in the tub. He and my kids were crying. Then when the ambulance got there, the police was with them. They told me if I agreed to get help they wouldn't take my kids. God was still showing me favor and I am still learning why He loves me like He does. I'm truly grateful. *For surely, O LORD, you bless the righteous; you surround them with your favor as with a shield* --Psalms 5:12. God told old death to behave. Jesus had the keys and He released me right when I asked for Him. Did I walk in that? No, not at first. I really wanted to do better, I just didn't know how to really do it. You see, the enemy does not want to give up without a fight.

To anyone reading this and you don't think you can make it, you can. Just hold on to Jesus, He will never leave nor forsake you. God works everything out for our good. Just hold on to His hand and He will see you through. *Keep your lives free from the love of money and be content with what you have, because God has said, "Never will I leave you; never will I forsake you"* --Hebrews 13:5.

Even though I was really trying to go to church, I just could not leave my past behind me. Conquering addiction is not easy but I was determined not to give up. My struggle continued throughout the years. Then the attack started on my children. I started hanging with a younger man one night and the police called while I was out with him in Richmond, which was about thirty minutes away from my home. They said my children were in the back of their police car because they had allowed one of their friends to talk them into going outside late at night to go down the street and flatten tires. Now the enemy is attacking my children, so I rushed home.

But of course God told the enemy no he couldn't have my children. They never got into trouble again. Shortly after that we moved. The very next morning my class leader from church called me, talk about God's timing. She prayed for me and I went to bible study and then to church on Sunday, I went to church and I joined three choirs. Finally, I was truly serving God. Of course it wasn't easy, but I was determined to stay on course with Jesus. *But the seed on good soil stands for those with a noble and good heart, who hear the word, retain it, and by persevering produce a crop* --Luke 8:15.

~ *Chapter 15* ~

God always meets us right where we are. When I was a child I acted like a child. Now, the enemy tried to tempt me with a man in the church. Now do I believe that God wanted me to stumble? No, of course not, but it kept me interested in church. So He allowed something to peak my interest in the building. As I was growing in the word of God, and preoccupied with this man who flirted with me every chance he got, I stayed the course. *But grow in the grace and knowledge of our Lord and Savior Jesus Christ. To him be glory both now and forever! Amen* –2 Peter 3:18.

But that wasn't all I was doing. I was actually working hard now and, at the same time the enemy was trying to come between me and my walk with the Lord. My job was messing with my time but I made a decision to trust God. *Blessed is the man who perseveres under trial, because when he has stood the test, he will receive the crown of life that God has promised to those who love him* --James 1:12.

When they would schedule me to work on Sunday I would go to church in the morning and leave right after first service. My children were picked up by my mother and I would go back to get them after work. If I had bible study or choir rehearsal my job would schedule me to come in. So I decided to take this to the manager. They claimed that I told them I could work on those days which was a lie birthed out the pit of hell. The devil is a liar, I chose that day who I would serve.

The very next thing the enemy did was schedule me on the day my children were getting baptized. That was it. I quit. Now I was really putting my faith to work. I had to trust in the Lord with all my heart and lean not to my own understanding. *Trust in the LORD with all your heart and lean not on your own understanding;* --Proverbs 3:5.
On that beautiful day when my children were baptized, is when the Holy Spirit said fret not, and that's what I did. *Be still before the LORD and wait patiently for him; do not fret when men succeed in their ways, when they carry out their wicked schemes* --Psalms 37:7.

My unemployment was denied, but God had another plan. He has always been so faithful to me. I didn't compromise and God rewarded me for that one leap of faith. He sent another angel to tell me about a job assisting this wonderful hairstylist in Oakland.

God will always be there to meet us, if we step out on faith and trust Him. *Let us hold unswervingly to the hope we profess, for he who promised is faithful* --Hebrews 10:23. When I decided to move to my next house the man I was interested in from church asked if he could move in with me. He said his landlords were tripping with him. I knew for a fact that he was behind on his rent. Looking back, the enemy thought he would keep me under his yoke of bondage but God allowed him to do everything he did for God's purpose. The word of God says He allows good and evil for His purpose.

When we moved into the new house as a family, I thought it would be that way, but that was far from the truth. For anyone reading this book, never allow a man to use you, especially when they claim to be ministers of the gospel of Jesus Christ. God will only allow so much before He steps in and cleans up house. *He will sit as a refiner and purifier of silver; he will purify the Levites and refine them like gold and silver. Then the LORD will have men who will bring offerings in righteousness,* --Malachi 3:3.

When I started to go back to my old ways, craving drugs again, that is when I told him he had to go. I can't forget how his face changed shape that night as I was talking to him. It was like he was a real demon. He was sitting on the couch trying to chastise my kids. How are you going to chastise someone when you know you are not right. When I wrote him a letter that night and told him it was time to really leave, it got real crazy because he got so angry. We were in the dark and as he was arguing, his face contorted like those people in the movie "The Devils Advocate," it was scary. God has not given us a spirit of fear but of power, love and a sound mind.

When he woke up the next morning he found somewhere else to go. When he moved out my heart was broken and I started getting high again. I know you probably ask why? It's like every time something traumatic happened, I would resort to my old ways. The word of the Lord says a fool returning to his old ways is like a dog returning to his own vomit. *As a dog returns to its vomit, so a fool repeats his folly* --Proverbs 26:11.
No person has the same walk with the Lord. Everyone has their own mountain to climb and mountain to move.

It seemed easier to go back to the familiar than to trust God, stay at home and wait on Him. I didn't want to be lonely. I was really a baby in Christ and I wanted to stay with God but just didn't have the strength to do it back then.

I remember calling in to work trying to get out of coming in but I had to go in anyway. I had been up all night and it was the most humiliating thing that I ever experienced. God allows situations and circumstances to come because He has greatness in store for you. So you will go through the fire but you won't get burned. *When you pass through the waters, I will be with you; and when you pass through the rivers, they will not sweep over you. When you walk through the fire, you will not be burned; the flames will not set you ablaze* --Isaiah 43:2. I was out for two days again on dope and I needed to go to the store on the way home but the Holy Ghost kept telling me to get off the freeway at this particular exit. But did I listen? *I will instruct you and teach you in the way you should go; I will counsel you and watch over you* --Psalms 32:8. I got into a car accident that morning. God spared my life but it was time for me to put my trust in the Lord for real now. My car was totaled out.

To God be the glory. He took His finger and shook me up that morning. At first I was renting cars for a very short period of time then I was catching the bus everyday for six months after. I ran out of rent, a car, money and it wasn't easy. But I never stopped going to church, choir rehearsal, or bible study. I stopped getting high again without question. I remember standing at the bus stop and I looked up. I said to God I was sorry. I felt that if something didn't change I was going to lose my mind. God is so amazing and we are so spoiled. We think we can't go without, but He carries us the whole time.

He never answered me that morning, but about a month later, because I never stopped believing and never stopped serving, He moved according to my faith and obedience. I would spend the night at my mom's house so I would be on time for church on Sunday mornings. It was all right at first, but women know that after a while you and mom stop getting along especially when they don't walk the same walk of faith as you do.

After many failed trials at trying to get a car on my own, God sent another angel--my son's grandmother. I know it was God because she and I knew that she never would have done anything like that for somebody else. Not only did she cosign, but when they asked her to put the car in her name because she had great credit, she did it!

Look at God. Just when you think you won't have any help, He sends you some help. He even makes your enemies be at peace with you. Even though she was my son's grandmother she really didn't like me very much. God moved on her heart and that's just how good God is. All powerful, Almighty God!!!

He did exceedingly and abundantly above all I could ask or think. *Now to him who is able to do immeasurably more than all we ask or imagine, according to his power that is at work within us,* --Ephesians 3:20. Now I had a brand new minivan, beautiful with wood grain, and CD player. All my children could fit comfortably in it. Look at God. She said that when she got up that morning God told her she would be helping someone, she just didn't think it would be like that and it would be me. I am still driving that car now.

A few years later I fell on hard times and got behind on the note a few months. Not only did she pay the notes and allowed me to repay her a little at a time but eventually she decided to just go ahead and pay the car off. Look at God, He never fails to do something to always blow your mind.

~ *Chapter 16* ~

So here I am and God has reminded me of the call on my life. Yes in a still small voice He says to peach His word. I was still working, still singing in the choir, then I stepped out on faith and did what is the scariest thing of all. I went to the altar and confessed that the Lord has called me to preach. Anyone who knows what that feels like, knows that it is hard. You deal with all sorts of emotions and fears, you don't feel worthy of the call. Then if you know your word, you know to whom much is given, much is required.

Then of course, the enemy tries to attack again. I have to make this clear. The enemy can't do anything unless God allows him to. What was to come next was only a test.

The woman where I worked asked me to leave. She said I was pushing too hard and I was always talking about Jesus too much to the clients. Now to this day I still don't understand or not clear as to why she would say something like that to me. We both professed to love Christ. He was supposed to be Lord over our lives. So how could I possibly be pushing too hard when I would talk to my other co-worker and clients about their relationship with the Lord. Anyway it broke my heart, especially since it was two weeks before Christmas. Talk about hitting you beneath the belt. Not to mention the concern for the kids because it was Christmas time. Now there were only a few things in my life that were stable and my job and children were two of them. *But you, O God, do see trouble and grief; you consider it to take it in hand. The victim commits himself to you; you are the helper of the fatherless* --Psalms 10:14. Our Father was so faithful to His word, that He would never leave us nor forsake us. He already had a place for me to work before I even asked Him. Not only that, He put people in my life to bless my kids for Christmas because God knew I didn't have any money for them. I barely had money to pay bills. Glory to God for His favor and His blessings we don't even deserve, He is so faithful.

My life with Christ has been the most exciting thing that has ever happened to me. There were times I wanted to give up but He has always strengthened me to keep pressing forward to trust him and lean not to my understanding. So the closer I drew to Him, the closer He drew to me. I truly love the Lord, and He has always heard everyone of my cries. *Delight yourself in the LORD and he will give you the desires of your heart* --Psalms 37:4.

I left the salon, broken but not alone, heart-broken but not dead. I went from East Oakland to a salon on Broadway close to downtown. It was nice too. That was where my season changed again. I was a minister but still struggling with addiction. Wow, talk about your fiery trials, I was faking it to make it. I really wanted to please God but I didn't know who I was in Him at that time in my life. *You are my hiding place; you will protect me from trouble and surround me with songs of deliverance. Selah* --Psalms 32:7. I mean I had been struggling so long with drugs that now there was no room for parties, no room for mistakes with a responsibility to please God. I kept on making mistakes even though I really wanted to please my Father.

One time I was up all night and I had three clients coming in that morning at work, and two were going to prom. How selfish was that. I knew I had to go to work and they were counting on me but no, I wanted to party anyway. I felt so stupid because I was so hung over. The assistant and the owner wound up helping me because they knew what was wrong with me. I was so embarrassed again. Now I know God had to humble me because I was thinking too highly of myself as a minister. *Unless the Lord builds the house, its builders labor in vain. Unless the Lord watches over the city, the watchmen stand guard in vain* -- Psalms 127:1. *But he gives us more grace. That is why Scripture says: "God opposes the proud but gives grace to the humble." Submit yourselves, then, to God. Resist the devil, and he will flee from you* --James 4:6-7. There were so many times I did that but God knew I truly wasn't ready for the call. I heard it but I realize that it wasn't time for me to actually walk in it.

There is a great responsibility that comes with taking care of God's sheep. You have to live above reproach, with no room for any garbage. *Humble yourselves, therefore, under God's mighty hand, that he may lift you up in due time* --1Peter 5:6. Then it became unbearable to work there. However I didn't realize it was me. I went to the next assignment by Lake Merritt, which was a much nicer place and a great place to be. I had keys to come and go when I pleased. I could work as late as I needed or wanted to and it was truly a blessing. This place was small but it was just enough space for the three of us, the owner and one stylist. We worked well together for the most part. The owner was beautiful inside and out, but again I relapsed.

I was dysfunctional for a long time, story after story. However, I never stopped going to church, which brings me to this question. How many people across this nation can be in church and have an outward appearance of change but no real inner change? The answer is billions. That is because some ministry leaders really don't care.

They just want to see you show up for the head count, the tithe, offering and membership.

If you are reading this book and you know someone who is struggling with addiction and their walk with the Lord, pray for them, check on them because someone is just one heartbreak away from relapsing.

Don't stop praying, don't ever think God is too busy to hear or even answer your prayer because I'm a living testimony that He will and He does answer your prayers. *Pray continually;* --1Thessalonians 5:17.

Don't ever stop reading your word; it will penetrate to the very bone and marrow. *Do your best to present yourself to God as one approved, a workman who does not need to be ashamed and who correctly handles the word of truth --* 2Timothy 2:15. So as I come near the close of this book, I realize that everything I went through wasn't for me, it was to give a testimony for that one mother, that father, family member or friend, who was thought to be not worthy of God's love or the call on their life.

Realize that your testimony is your victory of God's mercy, His love and kindness towards us. He loves us so much that He sent His only son so we could have relationship with Him, so He could forgive us and cleanse our sins. He only knows how much we have truly sinned and fallen short.

Without faith it is impossible to please God, so never give up on your faith. Know that you know that all things work together for the good of them that love Him and are called according to His purpose. Yes, you have a purpose and don't you let no devil in hell tell you differently!

I went through a lot of clients at that point in my life, partly because I was unreliable. My word was no good. So I lost more clients than I've kept. I hurt a lot of people on my way to recovery. So if you're reading this book and you're one of them, please accept my humble, heartfelt apology. I'm truly sorry. I never meant to hurt any of you, I was really sick back then so I beg you to please forgive me.

God knew the work He was doing. I just didn't slow down enough to allow myself to be transformed by the renewing of my mind. *Do not conform any longer to the pattern of this world, but be transformed by the renewing of your mind. Then you will be able to test and approve what God's will is--his good, pleasing and perfect will* --Romans 12:2. I was so gone that I would really be looking for people under the bed like I was on crack. I didn't realize that I was under serious attack from the enemy. I had demons all around me. I could feel them moving in my presence. It was a trip, and as time went on it didn't get any better. I was paranoid all the time. I was high. So why did I continue to do it? It is very simple. My body would crave the drug. So even if I didn't want to get high I couldn't help myself.

God revealed that it was time for me to fight the fight of faith. *Fight the good fight of the faith. Take hold of the eternal life to which you were called when you made your good confession in the presence of many witnesses --* 1Timothy 6:12. I always thought people were trying to set me up or after me. It was so insane.

As I mentioned before there were two men that I knew were using me, but I thought I was using them. They would leave me in their house. These were two different houses, but two of the same type of demon. Now listen to this, they wouldn't stay up all night, but would get rest. They would leave me in the house alone. All the while they knew I would be searching through their things for more stuff. How crazy is that?

I didn't eat all day and to make matters worse I looked terrible. How could I possibly go outside looking like that? Well I didn't. I stayed in bondage to the house each day and when the sun would come up I went home before the children could really see what I looked like.

I would not wish that feeling on anyone. After I was used up, I would ask them to drive me home, but guess what, I couldn't walk out the door. Too paranoid. I was a mess. Thank God, He will take your mess and make it a miracle! I tried my best to keep my partying to the weekends but sometimes I would mess up and be out on Saturday. God was being so good. He would allow me to hear a word on the television. He's just that good. *Then they cried out to the Lord in their trouble, and he brought them out of their distress* --Psalms 107:28.

I am telling you about the goodness of the Lord in the midst of all my ups and downs with drugs and men. Moving on, I had a wonderful place to work and then I met another man. It seemed so right in the beginning but much to my surprise it turned out to be as bad as the rest of my past relationships. In the midst of everything God kept me from AIDS and HIV. *Though I walk in the midst of trouble, you preserve my life; you stretch out your hand against the anger of my foes, with your right hand you save me. The Lord will fulfill his purpose for me; your love, O Lord, endures forever-- do not abandon the works of your hands -* -Psalms 138:7-8.

This man and I had some very good times, and stayed in some of the nicest hotels. We went dancing every weekend. Anybody who knows me knows I love dancing, music and just plain good fun. But something was still missing. I thought that a good man would make my life complete, but it didn't because the best man I could of ever had was already there the whole time waiting for me to spend time with Him. That good man was Jesus, He was already standing there. *And the God of all grace, who called you to his eternal glory in Christ, after you have suffered a little while, will himself restore you and make you strong, firm and steadfast* --1Peter 5:10.

When I look back it was because I didn't trust Him, Jesus, and I always got in the way. I kept falling for the same trick of the enemy. I would always stop doing drugs long enough to get my face together, regain my weight and then I was right back at it. I know now that this was because I wanted to satisfy my flesh and not truly live a life pleasing unto God. *Therefore, I urge you, brothers, in view of God's mercy, to offer your bodies as living sacrifices, holy and pleasing to God--this is your spiritual act of worship* --Romans 12:1. I wasn't and didn't really know what the word Holy meant until a few years ago.

I heard but I never really saw many people living it. I know now that I needed time alone with God, and I needed to develop a relationship with Him, instead of the ones that always let me down.

Of course the new relationship was in trouble too. He had a drinking problem. He was a drunkard and I was still a dope fiend. We were always arguing because he got too drunk and even though I wasn't getting high at first, I was going through withdrawals. Then I really wanted to be married. Yeah I wanted to settle down. Now did I know what that really meant at the time? No. So I was pushing him away and he was getting on my nerves by always being drunk in public.

One day we had a conversation and he asked me why I was so moody all the time and I told him it was because I like to get high sometimes and I knew he didn't do that. Do you know what that fool said? He had the nerve to say it was alright as long as I did it with him. Just like a selfish man, not seeing this as a real serious issue, just knowing what's good to him. So instead of getting a person some help he would allow you to be dysfunctional.

Don't think for one minute that I didn't tell him that I was really trying to quit and it was a real problem for me. He just wanted what he wanted and didn't really care about my soul or my life. But that was the story of my life then. I was the fun girl, never a wife, always fun. Lord knows I hesitate to share all the intimate details of my life, but I know this will set the captives free.

After eight months I called it quits. I had enough and wasn't satisfied with just fun anymore. I wanted something more serious. Whenever life threw me a punch, I resorted to the same behavior over and over again.

I dated a few more men in and out of the church, just looking for love in all the wrong places. God was there the whole time waiting for me to receive His love. I know now that God is a jealous God. There shall be no other god's before Him. *For it is written: "Be holy, because I am holy."* --1Peter 1:16. That's what I had done. I had set up this idol of a husband, a demi god, and God was not having it. I know now that if I delight myself in Him, He will give me the desires of my heart. *Delight yourself in the LORD and he will give you the desires of your heart* --Psalms 37:4.

~ *Chapter 17* ~

After three years of living in Fremont I decided to make a change. Me and the kids moved to Antioch, California. I figured if I moved, things would change unaware that I was the one who needed to change. I was working in Berkeley, but there were issues at all of the locations. One salon was having financial problems, one was having family problems and the other was just having problems with their life. I went to work every day praying that I was going to make it straight home afterwards, but it didn't always work out that way.

Let me tell you, I worked in a salon that was right next door to a bar known for drugs. Most of the people I wanted to avoid seemed to always be there. I did my best for a moment, but of course you know my story, the same thing happened. It would be a man, a club, a problem, but the problem was me not the club. I started to mess up for real now on this job. People could tell my good days from my bad days. Being the needy person I was lonely, so I wanted and needed attention, and I would actually lower my standards time after time.

In addition, I was still grieving from my father's death. I really believed that all that stuff I was doing was who I was. That was untrue. I am a child of the most high God, He loves me, I'm His daughter, the apple of His eye. But I went through the motions with more crazy relationships, almost losing my job for real. I fail to mention that I was working in a Christian salon. They prayed for me, spent time in the word with me, and really tried to help me. After about a year, I left my home church with one of the ministers who starting her own church. At first it seemed as though I was going to make it this time but I was wrong. You see the church is full of sick people including leaders. It's like the hospital. If you want to be healed you can if you ask for the Lords help. If you don't earnestly receive God's love in your heart you will stay in the pain He wants to deliver you from. *If we confess our sins, he is faithful and just and will forgive us our sins and purify us from all unrighteousness* –1 John 1:9.

Just because I left that hospital didn't mean I was going to receive proper care in my new hospital. My new pastor allowed me to be the praise dance coordinator but I felt that I wasn't able to spread my wings. I believe I felt that way because the church was fairly new and at the time I was still broken. But by being broken, it seemed the children in my charge had more control that I did. I know now that it was a lie birthed out of the pit of hell because satan is the father of lies and a deceiver. So his job is to hit you when you're down and cause confusion. The battle is in your mind and that is where the war is fought. Thank God satan was already defeated on Calvary, yes he is a defeated foe. So when it felt like I wasn't being heard, now I know and believe that was a lie and my Pastor loved me. She has always had my best interest at heart. Thank you Pastor Scott. I love and appreciate everything you have always done for me and my family.

Moving on, my feelings were hurt then I met another man. Now this relationship was different, because I married him. Believe God when He says He knows the plans He has for you, plans to prosper you not to harm you. *For I know the plans I have for you," declares the LORD, "plans to prosper you and not to harm you, plans to give you hope and a future* --Jeremiah 29:11. Everything for a brief minute seemed to be all right but little did I know that he was on drugs and that demon was dying to drag me down with him. I was really stupid and blind because I married too quickly. There were warning signs I ignored. Now ask me why I didn't run when he asked me to marry him three days after we met. First red flag! Then he needed to move in right away. Second red flag! And the third red flag was his clothes were in garbage bags.

I married this man after knowing him for three months maybe four. Two weeks after he moved in the house, I told him that we couldn't live like this. I was not shacking up.

You're probably thinking that we were getting high first but we weren't. When he said let's go to Reno, I said OK, that was it. I didn't know he was getting high the whole time. Talk about a set up. I believed and thought he was going to be a good father to all of our children. Now there were ten kids combined--mine and his. He fooled me and all of our kids.

~ *Chapter 18* ~

As fate would have it we were married on September 9, 2002. We started off wrong to begin with. We had sex one time before we were married and were unequally yoked. He had no intentions of serving any form or fashion in the church or living a life dedicated to serving the Lord. He loved to get high all the time and lied about it. He was a security guard and worked the nightshift but always came home hyper.

I really ignored all the signs. He was not from God but I thought I could change him. I was wrong, he changed me, and I looked worse than I ever did in my entire life of drug use.

I stopped going to church because I started to miss the dance rehearsals, and I was the coordinator. Wrong, wrong, wrong! I'm so thankful to God for intervening after this man came into my life. After about six months of marriage, we got a divorce. Now I won't go into all the ugly details of demons, harlots and drugs, but let's just say what the devil meant for bad this time, God truly turned it to bless me.

God allowed the enemy to work through this man to get me to where I needed to be. *You intended to harm me, but God intended it for good to accomplish what is now being done, the saving of many lives* --Genesis 50:20. I was torn down, heart broken, tweaked out, unstable in all my ways, but every tear I cried and every prayer I prayed God heard them. He not only removed him, He also set me free from drug addiction. *In righteousness you will be established: Tyranny will be far from you; you will have nothing to fear. Terror will be far removed; it will not come near you --* Isaiah 54:14.

As I sit here and write the closing pages to this book of my life, relationships, failures, and successes, I'm completely drug free and alcohol free. You see God sustained me until I got to a place of being so desperate for Him. If I got high one more time I would have died in that sinful state. I had so many relationships during the process of healing and recovery, but one thing I do know is that satan is like a roaring lion seeking whom he can devour.

If you don't know how to put on the full amour of God you'd better learn. This race is not given to the swift but to the one who endures to the end. *Do you not know that in a race all the runners run, but only one gets the prize? Run in such a way as to get the prize* –1 Corinthians 9:24. The road is very narrow and only a few make it, but because of the precious blood of Jesus, we are free, and we have forgiveness. *But small is the gate and narrow the road that leads to life, and only a few find it* --Matthew 7:14.

The Word of God in 2 Chronicles 7:14 says, if My people who are called by My name would humble themselves, pray, seek My face, turn from their wicked ways then I will hear from heaven, forgive them of their sins and I would heal their land. That's all we have to do, is turn, turn to Him, our Father, His son. They love us so much and we were sent the Comforter, the Holy Spirit. Wow, what a mighty God we serve.

All we have to do is truly and sincerely ask for help and God will give it to us. So I am thankful for my new church family. I've been at Grace Bible Fellowship for four years now. This is where I received my healing and God's true love relationship with Him. I remember being so high and all I could do was want more drugs, but now all I want is more Jesus. I love everyone who helped to get me to this point of being complete and whole. I never knew what it was like to be whole but now I do. *My people are destroyed from lack of knowledge. "Because you have rejected knowledge, I also reject you as my priests; because you have ignored the law of your God, I also will ignore your children* --Hosea 4:6. So whoever you are, wherever you are, never give up on God because He never gives up on us.

Thank You God. I'm Truly Free! *So if the Son sets you free, you will be free indeed.* --John 8:36.

~ *Epilogue* ~

Then the LORD said to me, "Write my answer in large, clear letters on a tablet, so that a runner can read it and tell everyone else. --Habbakuk 2:2

What the devil meant for bad, you God would turn it around to bless me. During the course of writing this assignment, I have had many highs and a whole lot of lows. One thing for certain, God truly had His hands on me. Every step was ordered by the Lord for such a time as this.

Since the completion of this book I have transitioned from one vineyard to another. I would like to thank Bishop Carl C. Smith and Lady Adrienne Smith of New Birth in Pittsburg, California. You didn't know it sir, but your words to close out the year 2010 forever changed my life. They captivated me, because God knew where He was taking me and He also knew I was hungry for the real meat and potatoes of the Word. I desire a deeper relationship with the King, the Father and His Holy Spirit. Thank you for being a gentleman just like our Father and asking me if you could be my pastor. Without hesitation I said yes.

So it begins. I have entered into a land flowing with milk and honey. God answered my prayers when He sent me to my very own Joshua, Lakesha Smith--My sister, my girlfriend, my sharpener, my accountability partner. My sparing partner, you are my little engine that could. Without the countless hours spent on the phone in prayer and confessions, I never would have transitioned into my wealthy place. I love you sister!!! You are truly special, and you will never know how much I love and appreciate everything you poured into me. Pushing me, encouraging me, always telling me "It's going to be alright," "now let's move forward," "What are we going to change so that we don't end up here again."

I don't know if you knew it, but God used you to help me stand when I couldn't stand alone. "Well done, thy good and faithful servant." You were and still are your sister's keeper. You helped me to keep my eyes fixed on the problem solver, Jesus. Thank you Kesh, love you so much.

A special thanks to Alfonzo Tucker, author of "Noises." And thank you to my Exotic Faces family: LaShaun Fields, co-worker and to Dee and David McClain, owners. "Now the first shall be last and the last shall be first"... to Momma Chris, there are no words to express all you have given and poured into me and this book. I Love You. You were faithful from start to finish. God's got a blessing with your name on it!

Now to all my haters, back-bitters, doubters, gossipers, liars, and betrayers...Thank you. God used you to keep me on my knees and in His face. He used you to keep me in prayer. Without all of you breaking my heart, letting me down, persecuting me, I wouldn't have needed Him that much more. He said that He would keep me in the midst of my enemies, and that's exactly what He did. I love you all for allowing Him to use you to get me where He wanted me, totally submitted to His will. The very thing that I thought would kill me made me stronger. I will be forever grateful to all of you. Bless you. Thank you. It is finished, in Jesus name. Amen!

~ *About the Author* ~

Constance Cooper was born and raised in the spring of 1972 in Richmond, California. Now the single mother of four beautiful children, she is a cosmetologist, make up artist by profession and a lover of fashion--she loves her shoes and handbags.

Constance has been a member of First A.M.E. Church where she rededicated her life to God, and Tree of Life Empowerment Ministries, in Oakland, CA. She then received her healing and deliverance at Grace Bible Fellowship in Antioch, CA. As a new member of New Birth Church of Pittsburgh, California, she has never been interested in titles. "I believe titles have some how corrupted a lot of very anointed pastors, ministers, evangelists, psalmists and every other title you can think of," she says.

Constance is living for Christ everyday now serving as a praise dance, choir member and minister of the Gospel of Jesus Christ. Loving God and His children, she desires to help and save the lost with a passion to make the young, as well as mature women, see how beautiful they truly are inside and out. Conscious that only God knows what will take place in her life and where He is taking her, she maintains a willingness to go. "With Christ all things are possible."

Constance cherishes the time she spends with God in His Word, His Presence, and His love. Among her other passions is family, wholeness and growing in His Word together and allowing Him to direct their paths through faith. "For without faith it is impossible to please God."

She desires to please Him by being transparent in order to get the lost to believe that there is still hope for them. Through the testimony of "The Chronicles of Connie," she endeavors to give that hope to a lost and dying world--that with Jesus we all have hope, because our hope is in Him and that they will be free just like her. "For whom the Son sets free is free indeed."

"Thank you Jesus for setting me free. I love you all," says Constance Cooper.

How to Contact the Author
"The Chronicles of Connie"

Constance Cooper

Email: connieantioch@yahoo.com

Website: www.thechroniclesofconnie.weebly.com

NOTES

Made in the USA
Lexington, KY
08 June 2011